Skiathos Travel Guide 2025

Uncover Coastal Adventures, Outdoor Activities, Beaches, and Natural Heritage

Roberto J. Spivey

To easily explore Skiathos, simply scan the QR Code with your Smartphone and access interactive Maps.

Table of Contents

Chapter 1: Introduction to Skiathos 6

My Love Affair with Skiathos: A Personal Journey...........................8

1.1 Geographical Overview and Location..13

1.2 Historical Journey Through Time 17

1.3 Modern-Day Skiathos: Culture and Society 22

1.4 Best Times to Visit: Understanding Seasonal Changes..............27

Chapter 2: Planning Your Journey 32

2.1 Getting to Skiathos: Transportation Options...........................32

2.2 Visa Requirements and Entry Procedures................................37

2.3 Accommodation Guide by Region and Budget..........................41

2.4 Suggested Itineraries: From Weekend Breaks to Extended Stays
....48

2.5 Travel Insurance and Health Considerations............................53

Chapter 3: Discovering Skiathos Town..58

3.1 Navigating the Old Town's Architecture..................................58

3.2 The Port Area and Waterfront Experience 63

3.3 Shopping Districts and Local Markets 67

3.4 Cultural Landmarks and Museums...72

3.5 Evening Entertainment and Nightlife Spots.............................77

Chapter 4: Beaches and Coastal Adventures...................................82

4.1 Mapping the Golden Coastline 82

4.2 Signature Beaches: From Koukounaries to Lalaria 87

4.3 Water Sports and Maritime Activities *92*

4.4 Hidden Coves and Secluded Spots *97*

4.5 Beach Facilities and Accessibility Guide *102*

Chapter 5: Natural Heritage and Outdoor Activities **108**

5.1 The Pine Forest Ecosystem *108*

5.2 Hiking Trails and Walking Routes *113*

5.3 Bird Watching and Wildlife Observation *118*

5.4 Photography Locations and Viewpoints *123*

5.5 Environmental Conservation Efforts *128*

Chapter 6: Culinary Journey **134**

6.1 Traditional Skiathian Cuisine *134*

6.2 Restaurant Guide by Region *138*

6.3 Local Produce and Markets *143*

6.4 Cooking Classes and Food Experiences *147*

6.5 Wine and Spirit Tasting Opportunities *151*

Chapter 7: Cultural Immersion **156**

7.1 Religious Heritage and Monastery Tours *156*

7.2 Traditional Festivals and Celebrations *161*

7.3 Arts and Crafts Scene *165*

7.4 Local Customs and Etiquette *170*

7.5 Language Guide: Essential Greek Phrases...................*175*

Chapter 8: Practical Information **180**

8.1 Banking and Currency Exchange *180*

8.2 Communication Services and Internet Access *185*

8.3 Medical Facilities and Pharmacies *190*

8.4 Transportation Around the Island *195*

8.5 Sustainable Tourism Practices *199*

Conclusion: Your Skiathos Journey **204**

Reflections on Island Life *204*

Appendices **210**

A. Annual Event Calendar *210*

B. Emergency Contacts and Important Numbers *215*

C. Ferry and Flight Schedules *220*

D. Packing Checklist by Season *224*

Chapter 1: Introduction to Skiathos

My Love Affair with Skiathos: A Personal Journey

The moment my feet touched Skiathos soil, I knew this wasn't going to be just another Mediterranean getaway. The warm breeze carried hints of pine and sea salt, wrapping around me like a gentle welcome from an old friend. This unexpected romance with a Greek island began right there at the small but bustling airport, where the runway practically kisses the Aegean Sea.

I remember standing at the arrival gate, watching seabirds glide past against a backdrop of mountains draped in emerald pine forests. The contrast was immediate and striking –

nature's raw beauty meeting modern convenience in perfect harmony. My taxi driver, Kostas, became my first window into island life, regaling me with stories passed down through generations of Skiathians as we wound our way through roads that revealed new wonders at every turn.

The island surprised me constantly. Each morning brought a new discovery: hidden pathways leading to secret beaches, ancient monasteries perched on clifftops telling silent stories of faith and perseverance, and village squares where time seemed to move at its own peaceful pace. I found myself falling into the rhythm of island life, where breakfast could stretch into lunch as I chatted with local café owners about their grandmother's secret recipes.

My wanderings through Skiathos Town became a daily adventure. The old port, with its centuries-old stones worn smooth by countless footsteps, led me through a maze of narrow streets where bougainvillea cascaded over whitewashed walls. Here, I discovered family-run tavernas where three generations worked side by side, serving dishes that tasted of sun-ripened tomatoes and herbs picked fresh from hillside gardens.

The beaches – oh, the beaches! Each one had its own personality. Koukounaries, with its pristine golden sand and crystal-clear waters, became my morning sanctuary. I'd arrive early, watching the sun paint the sky in watercolor hues while local fishermen pulled in their morning catch. Then there was hidden Lalaria, accessible only by boat, where white pebbles created an otherworldly landscape against turquoise waters. The boat trip there became an adventure in itself, with dolphins occasionally accompanying us through the waves.

But it wasn't just the physical beauty that captured my heart. It was the people – their warmth, their stories, their unwavering hospitality. Maria, who ran a small pottery shop in the old town, taught me about traditional crafts passed down through generations. She showed me how to shape clay the way her grandmother had taught her, each piece telling a story of island tradition.

I learned to slow down and appreciate simple pleasures: the way sunset turned the harbor waters to liquid gold, the sound of church bells echoing across the valleys, the taste of fresh-caught fish grilled to perfection at a beachside taverna. Every meal became a celebration, every conversation an opportunity to learn something new about this enchanting place.

The island's rhythms began to shape my days. Mornings might find me hiking ancient donkey trails through pine-scented forests to reach remote monasteries, where kind-faced monks shared stories of the island's spiritual heritage. Afternoons were spent discovering secluded coves or learning traditional dances at impromptu celebrations in village squares.

My most memorable evening came unexpectedly at a small festival in a mountain village. The sounds of bouzouki music filled the air as locals and visitors alike joined hands in traditional dances. An elderly woman grabbed my hand, pulled me into the circle, and with patient smiles and gentle guidance, taught me steps that had been danced on this island for centuries. That night, under stars that seemed close enough to touch, I understood why people fall deeply in love with Skiathos.

This guide emerged from those experiences – from countless conversations with locals, from early morning hikes to hidden viewpoints, from lazy afternoons exploring secret beaches, and from evenings spent in vibrant village squares. It's filled with practical advice, yes, but more importantly, it's infused with real experiences and genuine connections that made my time on Skiathos unforgettable.

I've written this guide to help you experience Skiathos not just as a destination, but as a living, breathing community with its own heartbeat and soul. You'll find detailed information about beaches, restaurants, and activities, but also insights into the island's character – the hidden spots where magic happens, the best times to visit certain places, and ways to connect with local culture that go beyond typical tourist experiences.

Through these pages, I'll share the secrets I discovered: where to find the best souvlaki in town (hint: it's not where most tourists go), which hiking trails offer the most spectacular views, and how to experience the authentic soul of Skiathos that exists beyond its famous beaches and bustling harbor.

This isn't just another travel guide – it's a companion for your own Skiathos adventure, born from real experiences and genuine love for this remarkable island. Whether you're planning your first visit or returning for the tenth time, I hope these insights help you create your own unforgettable memories on this magical Greek island. Let me show you the Skiathos I discovered, the one that stole my heart and continues to call me back year after year.

1.1 Geographical Overview and Location

Imagine sailing across the sparkling Aegean Sea, approximately 41°10'N and 23°29'E, where you'll discover Skiathos - the westernmost pearl of the Sporades archipelago. This small yet captivating Greek island emerges from the waters like a green jewel, spanning just 12 kilometers in length and 6 kilometers across at its widest point. Despite its modest size of 49.9 square kilometers, Skiathos packs an incredible variety of landscapes into its compact dimensions.

The island's position creates a natural gateway to the Sporades chain, sitting closest to mainland Greece among its sister islands. Looking east, you'll spot Skopelos shimmering on the horizon, while the Greek mainland's Port of Volos beckons from the west, a mere 76 kilometers away. This strategic location has shaped Skiathos's role as both a vital maritime crossroads and a welcoming first stop for travelers venturing into the Sporades.

Picture a butterfly that has gently landed on the sea - this mirrors Skiathos's distinctive shape. The island's northern and southern coasts tell dramatically different stories. The north coast stands proud and defiant, with rugged cliffs plunging dramatically into deep waters, shaped by millennia of winter winds. Here, the legendary Lalaria Beach showcases the raw power of nature, with its smooth white pebbles and towering chalk cliffs creating an almost otherworldly landscape.

In contrast, the southern coast opens its arms wide with gentle slopes and sheltered bays, home to more than 60 beaches of golden sand. This natural protection from the northern winds has made the south coast ideal for human settlement since ancient times. The coastline stretches an impressive 44 kilometers, creating countless hidden coves and beach havens waiting to be explored.

The island's backbone consists of two main mountains: Karafiltzanaka rising to 433 meters and Kounistra reaching 397 meters. These peaks aren't merely scenic features; they play a crucial role in the island's ecosystem. Their presence forces moisture-laden air upward, creating a unique microclimate that sustains Skiathos's remarkably dense pine forests, which cover about 80% of the island.

These forests are particularly special, composed primarily of Aleppo pines whose deep roots help prevent soil erosion on the island's many slopes. The trees extend their branches almost to the water's edge in many places, creating a rare and stunning marriage of forest and sea. This verdant coverage has earned Skiathos its reputation as the greenest island in the Sporades.

The island's geology tells an ancient story of volcanic activity and tectonic movements. The bedrock consists mainly of schist and limestone, minerals that sparkle with flecks of mica in the Mediterranean sun. This geological foundation creates natural springs and helps shape the island's fertile soil, perfect for growing the olive trees and fruit orchards that dot the landscape.

Water has played a master sculptor's role in shaping Skiathos. Seasonal streams have carved peaceful valleys through the terrain, creating natural pathways that have served as roads and hiking trails for generations. The largest of these valleys runs from Kanapitsa to Vromolimnos, creating a natural corridor that connects different parts of the island.

The island's position and topography work together to create a climate that draws visitors year-round. Sheltered by mountains from the cold northern winds in winter, while enjoying cooling sea breezes in summer, Skiathos maintains pleasant temperatures throughout the year. The island averages 280 days of sunshine annually, with summer temperatures typically ranging from 25°C to 35°C, while winter sees mild temperatures between 7°C and 15°C.

Accessibility to Skiathos mirrors its welcoming nature. The island's airport, with its famous runway extending into the sea, handles direct flights from major European cities during peak season. The well-protected port, nestled in the naturally curved bay of Skiathos Town, welcomes ferries year-round, connecting the island to both mainland Greece and neighboring islands.

The combination of these geographical elements - the protective mountains, the dense forests, the diverse coastline, and the strategic location - creates an island that feels both intimate and expansive. Each geographic feature contributes to Skiathos's unique character, from its climate to its ecosystems, making it a microcosm of Mediterranean beauty compressed into a small but perfect package.

1.2 Historical Journey Through Time

Walking through Skiathos today, every stone and pathway whispers stories of an island that has witnessed over 5,000 years of human history. Our journey begins in the Late Bronze Age, around 1200 BCE, when the first settlers established themselves on what is now called Kefala, a naturally fortified hill offering clear views across the Aegean waters. These early inhabitants left behind fragments of their lives – pottery shards, stone tools, and the foundations of simple dwellings that archaeologists continue to study today.

The Classical period marked Skiathos's emergence as a significant maritime power. By the 5th century BCE, the island's strategic position made it invaluable during the Persian Wars. In 480 BCE, the island played a crucial role in Greece's defense against Xerxes' invasion, serving as a critical warning station. The ancient Greeks had devised an ingenious system of fire signals stretching from Skiathos to Artemision, alerting Greek forces about Persian movements. Remnants of these signal towers still crown several hilltops, offering modern visitors panoramic views and a tangible connection to this pivotal moment in history.

The island flourished during the 4th century BCE under Athenian influence. This golden age saw the construction of the ancient city, whose ruins lie beneath modern Skiathos Town. Archaeological excavations have revealed sophisticated urban planning, with paved streets, public buildings, and a thriving port. The discovery of numerous amphorae suggests extensive trade networks stretching across the Mediterranean.

Roman rule brought new architectural styles and cultural influences. The Romans appreciated Skiathos's fine harbors and established several villas along the southern coast. Near modern-day Vromolimnos, visitors can still see the remains of a Roman bathhouse, its marble floors telling tales of luxury and sophistication.

The Byzantine era transformed the island's religious landscape. Between the 7th and 14th centuries, numerous monasteries were built, including the spectacular Evangelistria Monastery, which still stands today. Built in 1794, this monastery played a remarkable role in Greek history – it was here that fighters of the Greek Revolution took their oaths and where the first Greek flag was woven and blessed in 1807. Walking through its stone corridors today, you can almost hear the whispered prayers and revolutionary plans that once filled these halls.

However, Skiathos's position as a maritime crossroads also made it vulnerable. The medieval period saw repeated raids by pirates, forcing the inhabitants to abandon their coastal settlements for the safety of Kastro, a natural fortress on the island's northern tip. Built in the 14th century, Kastro became their home for nearly 400 years. Today, climbing the ancient path to Kastro reveals dramatic ruins of houses, churches, and fortifications perched precariously on the clifftop – a testament to human resilience in the face of constant threat.

The Ottoman period left its mark through architectural elements and cultural influences still visible in older buildings around Skiathos Town. The island's shipbuilding industry flourished during this time, with Skiathos's shipyards producing vessels renowned throughout the Mediterranean. The traditional boatyards (tarseranas) near the old port preserve this shipbuilding heritage.

The Greek Revolution of 1821 saw Skiathos emerge as a crucial base for revolutionary forces. The island's protected harbors sheltered Greek ships, while its forests provided timber for shipbuilding. The Evangelistria Monastery became a sanctuary for freedom fighters and a symbol of resistance.

The 19th and early 20th centuries brought both prosperity and challenges. The development of shipping and trade enriched many families, leading to the construction of the magnificent captain's houses that still line the streets of Skiathos Town. These neoclassical mansions, with their distinctive architecture and decorative elements, tell stories of maritime wealth and cultural sophistication.

Modern Skiathos began to emerge in the 1960s with the first waves of tourism. The island's natural beauty and rich heritage attracted visitors, spurring development while challenging the community to balance progress with preservation. Notable sites like the house of celebrated author Alexandros Papadiamantis, preserved as a museum, connect visitors to the island's more recent cultural history.

Each layer of history has left its imprint on Skiathos, creating an island where ancient ruins share space with medieval monasteries and neoclassical mansions. Archaeological sites continue to yield new discoveries, adding pieces to our understanding of this remarkable island's past. Modern Skiathos stands as a living museum, where history isn't just preserved in artifacts and ruins but lives on in traditions, architecture, and the daily rhythms of island life.

1.3 Modern-Day Skiathos: Culture and Society

Today's Skiathos presents a fascinating blend of traditional Greek island life and contemporary Mediterranean culture. With a year-round population of approximately 6,800 residents, the island transforms dramatically between seasons, swelling to over 30,000 people during peak summer months. This seasonal rhythm shapes every aspect of local life, from economic patterns to social interactions.

The island's permanent residents represent a diverse mix of age groups, though there's a noticeable trend of younger Skiathians returning home after university studies in Athens or abroad. This reverse migration brings fresh perspectives and international experience while maintaining strong connections to local traditions. Many young entrepreneurs have launched innovative businesses that respect traditional practices while embracing modern approaches – like family-owned restaurants incorporating contemporary cooking techniques into generations-old recipes.

Tourism undeniably drives Skiathos's modern economy, accounting for about 70% of local income. However, unlike some Greek islands that completely transform during tourist season, Skiathos maintains strong traditional economic activities. Local fishing fleets still head out before dawn, supplying restaurants with fresh catches. Small-scale olive oil production continues in centuries-old groves, and several families maintain beehives producing distinctive pine honey from the island's abundant forests.

The social structure revolves around extended family networks, with multiple generations often living close together or sharing business responsibilities. Morning coffee rituals at local kafeneia remain sacred social occasions where news spreads and community decisions take shape. These gatherings represent more than simple social events – they're the invisible threads keeping the community connected throughout rapid changes.

Education plays a central role in modern Skiathian society. The island's schools maintain high academic standards while incorporating local history and traditions into their curriculum. Students learn traditional dances alongside computer skills, and environmental education focuses on preserving the island's unique ecosystem. The local cultural center offers year-round programs teaching traditional crafts, music, and cooking to both residents and visitors.

Housing reflects the evolution of island life. Traditional stone houses with red-tiled roofs stand alongside modern apartments, though strict building codes preserve architectural harmony. Many families have adapted ancestral homes to include separate tourist accommodations, creating a unique dynamic where visitors become temporary members of extended family networks.

The relationship between locals and tourism reveals fascinating adaptations. Unlike the artificial "tourist shows" found on larger islands, Skiathos's cultural events remain authentically local. Summer festivals traditionally celebrating saint's days or harvest times now welcome visitors, but the core ceremonies and celebrations maintain their traditional character. Locals take pride in sharing genuine cultural experiences rather than manufactured ones.

Modern technology meshes surprisingly well with island traditions. WiFi covers most public spaces, and many local businesses use social media effectively. However, technology serves rather than replaces traditional social patterns. WhatsApp groups organize traditional panigiri festivals, while Facebook helps coordinate community clean-up events and cultural preservation projects.

The culinary scene exemplifies this cultural balance. Traditional tavernas serve centuries-old recipes alongside new interpretations of Greek classics. Young chefs returning from international training bring fresh techniques while respecting local ingredients and flavors. Family recipes pass down through generations, now documented on iPads alongside handwritten notebooks.

Environmental consciousness runs deep in modern Skiathian society. Local initiatives focus on sustainable tourism, waste reduction, and protecting the island's natural beauty. Community groups organize regular beach cleanups, while schools run environmental education programs. This environmental awareness stems from traditional respect for the land rather than imported green initiatives.

Art and creativity flourish in contemporary Skiathos. Local galleries showcase both traditional crafts and modern artistic expressions. The island's strong literary tradition, dating back to acclaimed author Alexandros Papadiamantis, continues through writing workshops and poetry readings. Modern artists draw inspiration from traditional themes while exploring contemporary mediums.

Religious traditions remain vibrant in modern island life. Church attendance stays high, particularly among younger generations, but religious practice adapts to contemporary life. Holy week celebrations incorporate ancient traditions while accommodating modern schedules, and summer weddings blend traditional Orthodox ceremonies with international guest lists.

The working rhythm of Skiathos reflects this cultural duality. Winter months focus on community projects, cultural events, and preparation for the tourist season. Summer's intense pace brings economic opportunities while testing the community's ability to maintain its cultural authenticity. Yet Skiathians have learned to embrace both rhythms, finding strength in their adaptability.

Looking toward the future, Skiathos faces challenges in maintaining this delicate balance. Housing prices, influenced by international buyers, concern young locals wanting to remain on the island. Environmental pressures from increasing tourism test infrastructure and natural resources. However, the community's strong sense of identity and adaptability suggest these challenges will meet creative solutions rooted in both tradition and innovation.

1.4 Best Times to Visit: Understanding Seasonal Changes

Skiathos lives and breathes through distinct seasons, each writing its own chapter in the island's yearly story. Let me walk you through this rhythmic dance of time, where every month brings unique experiences waiting to be discovered.

January whispers with winter's quiet charm. Temperatures hover between 7-13°C, and rainfall decorates the pine forests with glistening droplets. The island belongs to its 6,800 permanent residents now. Local tavernas serve heartwarming fasolada (bean soup) and gather around wood-burning stoves.

While swimming might raise eyebrows, January offers peaceful walks through empty beaches and photography opportunities of dramatic winter seas. Hotel prices drop to their lowest, often 70% below peak rates.

February continues winter's embrace but hints at coming spring. The air warms slightly to 8-14°C, and almond trees burst into pink-white blossoms across the island. Morning frost occasionally dusts the highest peaks, creating magical landscapes. Local life centers around olive harvesting, and visitors can join families in this centuries-old tradition. The sea remains wild and powerful, perfect for storm watching from cozy cafes in Skiathos Town.

March arrives with spring's first breath, temperatures climbing to 10-17°C. The island awakens as wildflowers carpet the hillsides. Early birds begin arriving – mainly Northern European retirees seeking extended stays. Hiking conditions become ideal, and trails through the pine forests release intoxicating aromas after rain showers. Some seasonal restaurants reopen, testing new menu items before the busy season.

April paints the island in vibrant colors. Temperatures reach 14-20°C, and the sea begins warming to swimmable conditions. Easter often falls in this month, transforming Skiathos with candlelit processions and midnight celebrations. Tourist numbers remain low, making this an ideal time for authentic cultural experiences. Accommodation prices stay reasonable, and you'll find locals eager to share spring traditions.

May heralds the pre-season sweet spot. Temperatures settle between 17-24°C, and the sea reaches a pleasant 20°C. The island buzzes with preparation energy as seasonal workers return. Beach bars begin opening, but crowds remain thin. Perfect conditions for outdoor activities attract rock climbers and mountain bikers. Prices begin their gradual climb but remain 30-40% below peak rates.

June brings summer's first wave, with temperatures ranging from 20-28°C and sea temperatures reaching 23°C. Tourist numbers build steadily, predominantly families with pre-school children and young couples. All facilities operate fully now, but you'll still find peaceful moments at remote beaches. The Lighthouse Festival draws international DJs, adding contemporary rhythm to traditional summer celebrations.

July blazes with peak summer energy. Temperatures soar to 23-33°C, and the sea feels like warm silk at 25°C. The island pulses with international visitors, primarily from UK, Germany, and Scandinavian countries. Beach clubs pump music across Koukounaries, and boats zip between beaches. Prices peak, and advance bookings become essential. Yet hidden coves still offer escape from the crowds.

August matches July's temperatures but amplifies the energy as Greeks arrive for their holidays. The Cultural Festival brings outdoor cinema, theater, and music performances. Every beach feels like a celebration, and nightlife reaches its zenith. Despite peak crowds, this month offers the most vibrant Greek cultural experiences as locals and tourists join in traditional summer panigiri festivals.

September whispers secrets to smart travelers. Temperatures gentle to 20-27°C, while the sea remains gloriously warm at 24°C. Crowds thin significantly after the first week, but all facilities remain open. Wine harvest begins, and visitors can join traditional grape-crushing celebrations. Prices drop by 30%, making this month a perfect blend of good weather, lower costs, and authentic experiences.

October paints with autumn's brush, temperatures ranging from 16-23°C. The sea holds summer's warmth at 21°C, perfect for swimming without crowds. Photography enthusiasts capture stunning sunsets, and hiking trails beckon with cool breezes. Local life resumes its slower pace, and visitors experience a more authentic island rhythm. Many seasonal restaurants offer end-of-season specials.

November brings the first winter rains, with temperatures between 12-18°C. The island exhales, settling into its off-season routine. Chestnuts fall in the forests, and mushroom hunting becomes a popular local activity. While some facilities close, enough remains open to support comfortable visits. Storm-watching becomes a dramatic spectacle from seafront cafes.

December wraps the island in winter stillness. Temperatures range from 8-15°C, with occasional storms creating powerful seascapes. Christmas brings unique local traditions, and visitors experience an intimate version of island life. While swimming becomes a polar bear activity, winter offers unique perspectives on Skiathos's beauty and culture.

Chapter 2: Planning Your Journey

2.1 Getting to Skiathos: Transportation Options

Reaching Skiathos mirrors the island's character - you can arrive in style by air or embrace the romance of a sea journey. Let me break down these pathways to paradise, sharing insights that go beyond typical travel listings.

Air Travel: The Direct Route

Skiathos International Airport "Alexandros Papadiamantis" welcomes visitors with one of the Mediterranean's most dramatic landings. The runway, stretching alongside crystal waters, handles both scheduled and charter flights. During peak season (May-October), direct flights connect Skiathos with London, Manchester, Amsterdam, Stockholm, Munich, and several other European hubs. Flight durations average 3-4 hours from most European cities.

British Airways and TUI operate regular services from London, with morning flights typically offering better value (average €180-250 one way). Scandinavian Airlines connects Stockholm and Copenhagen (€220-300), while Condor serves German cities (€200-280). Book these routes 4-6 months ahead, as prices can double closer to departure dates.

The shoulder seasons reveal a savvy traveler's secret: April and October flights often cost 40% less than peak fares, while still offering reliable weather. However, winter travelers need patience - the airport serves primarily domestic flights via Athens, operated by Olympic Air and Aegean Airlines.

The Athens Connection

Year-round access comes through Athens, with daily 35-minute flights by Olympic Air. Morning departures from Athens (around €80-120) allow smooth connections with international arrivals. A pro tip: the right-hand seats offer stunning views of the Sporades archipelago during approach.

Many travelers overlook the Athens route's flexibility. Missing a connection? The airport hotel offers day rates, and the express bus to Piraeus port (€5) opens up ferry options. I've turned such "mishaps" into memorable additions to the journey.

Sea Routes: A Journey Through History

Ferries connect Skiathos with several mainland ports, each offering unique advantages. The main routes operate from:

Volos: The closest major port, with year-round services by Hellenic Seaways. Fast ferries (2.5 hours, €38) run twice daily in summer, once daily in winter. The conventional ferry (4 hours, €28) offers a more leisurely pace and better sea views. Early morning departures provide magical sunrise scenes across the Pagasitic Gulf.

Agios Konstantinos: A shorter sea crossing (1 hour 40 minutes, €35) but requires longer land travel from Athens. Summer-only services make this ideal for combining island-hopping adventures. The port's small size means easier boarding procedures and shorter check-in times.

Thessaloniki: Weekly services in summer create interesting possibilities for northern Greece exploration. The overnight journey (8 hours, €45) saves on accommodation and delivers you to Skiathos at sunrise.

Combination Strategies

Smart planning opens up money-saving possibilities. Flying into Thessaloniki then taking the ferry can save €150-200 over peak-season direct flights. Similarly, Athens arrival followed by the scenic train to Volos (€18) creates an adventurous alternative to direct routes.

Seasonal Rhythms and Booking Wisdom

Summer demands advance planning. Ferry tickets become available 3-4 months ahead - book online through official websites rather than resellers. The Greece-specific quirk: ferry companies sometimes add extra services last-minute during peak demand, worth checking a week before travel.

Winter travelers should build flexibility into plans. Reduced schedules mean fewer options if weather affects services. December-February might see ferry cancellations during strong winds, though the airport rarely closes.

Arrival Insights

Morning arrivals offer smoother transitions - more taxi availability (fixed €15 fare to most locations) and less competition for port luggage storage (€5 per bag). The airport's compact size means quick exits, but summer afternoons can see queues at immigration.

The port area transforms through the day. Early arrivals find peaceful cafes perfect for orientation, while afternoon ferries dock amid the bustling promenade life. Both airport and port offer ATMs, but exchange rates improve in town.

Local Transport Connections

Upon arrival, resist rushing to your accommodation. The local bus system (€2 per ride) serves both port and airport effectively. Consider walking if staying in Skiathos Town - many hotels lie within 15 minutes of either arrival point, and the journey offers perfect orientation.

2.2 Visa Requirements and Entry Procedures

Planning Your Journey to Skiathos brings us to the vital matter of entry requirements - paperwork that often strikes anxiety into travelers' hearts. As someone who has crossed countless borders over decades of travel writing, I understand the importance of getting these details right. Let me walk you through the essentials of entering this Greek paradise in 2025.

The rules for entering Skiathos mirror Greece's broader entry policies as part of the Schengen Area. EU citizens enjoy the simplest path - they need only a valid national ID card or passport. The freedom of movement within the EU transforms what could be a bureaucratic headache into a straightforward arrival.

American, Canadian, British, and Australian passport holders can breathe easy - no visa is required for stays under 90 days. Your passport must remain valid for at least three months beyond your planned departure date. I recall arriving in Athens last summer, watching anxious travelers checking their passport expiry dates in the queue. Save yourself this stress by verifying your dates well in advance.

Citizens from non-EU countries requiring visas must submit their applications at Greek embassies or consulates in their home countries. The process typically takes 15 working days, though I advise allowing a month to account for unexpected delays. The standard Schengen visa fee stands at €80 for adults and €40 for children aged 6-12, while children under 6 enter free of charge.

The visa application demands several documents: a completed application form, passport photos, proof of travel insurance (covering medical expenses up to €30,000), round-trip flight reservations, hotel bookings, and bank statements demonstrating sufficient funds (approximately €50 per day of your stay). Your passport must have at least two blank pages and be no older than 10 years.

A crucial detail often overlooked: the Schengen Area's 90/180 day rule. This means you can stay for up to 90 days within any 180-day period. I've met countless travelers who misunderstood this rule, leading to uncomfortable situations at border control. Picture this: if you spent 60 days in Italy before flying to Skiathos, you'd only have 30 days remaining in your Schengen allowance.

Health and safety protocols evolve constantly. As of 2025, Greece maintains specific entry requirements regarding vaccination status and health documentation. You'll need to complete a Passenger Locator Form (PLF) before arrival, available on the Greek government's website. Submit this at least 24 hours before entry - I've seen travelers frantically filling forms on their phones at airports, which is far from ideal.

Long-term stays require additional preparation. If you're planning to spend more than 90 days in Skiathos, you'll need a national visa (type D). This process involves extra documentation, including proof of accommodation, comprehensive health insurance, and sometimes proof of employment or study enrollment. The processing time typically extends to 30 working days, and fees vary based on nationality and duration of stay.

Working holiday visas present another avenue for younger travelers from specific countries with bilateral agreements with Greece. These special arrangements typically allow stays of up to 12 months, though they come with strict age limits (usually 18-30) and quota restrictions.

Digital nomads eyeing Skiathos as their temporary office should note Greece's digital nomad visa initiative. This requires proof of remote work arrangements and minimum monthly income requirements - currently set at €3,500. The application process differs slightly from standard visas, with additional emphasis on proof of employment and income stability.

Entry requirements can change unexpectedly. During my decades of travel writing, I've learned to check official embassy websites even when I think I know the rules. The Greek Ministry of Foreign Affairs website remains your most reliable source for up-to-date information.

Keep copies of all your documents - both digital and physical. I store scans in a password-protected cloud folder and carry photocopies separate from my originals. This habit has saved countless travelers I've met over the years from serious complications when documents were lost or stolen.

Ultimately, while these requirements might seem daunting, they serve as your key to unlocking the treasures of Skiathos. Every form filled and document gathered brings you closer to experiencing the island's crystal waters and warm hospitality. In my experience, thorough preparation transforms border crossings from potential sources of anxiety into mere stepping stones on your journey to paradise.

2.3 Accommodation Guide by Region and Budget

Selecting the perfect place to stay in Skiathos shapes your entire island experience. I've spent countless nights in properties across this Greek paradise, from luxurious beachfront resorts to family-run guesthouses tucked away in olive groves. Let me share my intimate knowledge of the island's accommodations, region by region.

Skiathos Town - The Vibrant Heart

The island's capital presents a rich variety of accommodation choices. Along the old port, the Bourtzi Boutique Hotel (Skiathos Town, 37002; +30 24270 21304) occupies a privileged position. Rooms start at €180 per night in peak season, featuring modern amenities with traditional Aegean architecture. The rooftop terrace offers mesmerizing sunset views over the harbor. Their concierge service proves exceptionally helpful during busy periods.

A short walk from the harbor, Hotel Kostis (14 Papadiamantis Street; +30 24270 22950) represents excellent mid-range value. Summer rates begin at €120, including a generous breakfast featuring local products. The family running this establishment has maintained its authentic character while modernizing amenities. Air conditioning works flawlessly - crucial during July and August heat.

Budget travelers should consider Pension Marina (8 Evangelistrias Street; +30 24270 22730). Basic but clean rooms start at €65, with shared terraces overlooking winding alleyways. Despite its simplicity, the location proves unbeatable, and the owners' warmth compensates for any lacking luxuries.

Megali Ammos - Beach Paradise Minutes from Town

The prestigious Skiathos Princess Resort (Megali Ammos Beach; +30 24270 49731) sets the standard for luxury. Rates during high season reach €450 per night, but the experience justifies the investment. The private beach section, multiple swimming pools, and spa facilities create an oasis of comfort. Their children's program makes this especially attractive for families.

The nearby Megali Ammos House (Megali Ammos Beach Road; +30 24270 21171) offers a more intimate experience. Twelve individually designed rooms, starting at €160, combine modern comfort with traditional Greek style. The breakfast served on your private balcony, watching early morning swimmers, creates unforgettable memories.

Troulos - Family-Friendly Haven

Troulos Bay Hotel (Troulos Beach; +30 24270 49222) exemplifies the area's family-oriented atmosphere. Double rooms begin at €190 in peak season. The extensive gardens provide safe spaces for children, while adults appreciate the beachfront restaurant serving fresh seafood. Their half-board option offers excellent value during longer stays.

The charming Troulos Garden Studios (Troulos Main Road; +30 24270 49311) present a self-catering alternative. Units starting at €95 include well-equipped kitchenettes and spacious verandas. The owner, Maria, maintains a small vegetable garden, often sharing fresh produce with guests - a gesture that perfectly captures Greek hospitality.

Koukounaries - Natural Beauty and Luxury

Elivi Skiathos (Koukounaries Beach; +30 24270 49000) represents the pinnacle of island luxury. Summer rates start at €550, but the experience proves transformative. The resort seamlessly integrates with its protected natural surroundings. Their private beach sections, infinity pools, and sophisticated dining options attract discerning travelers seeking seclusion.

Mandraki Village Boutique Hotel (Koukounaries Road; +30 24270 49301) offers a more accessible luxury experience. Rooms from €230 feature elegant décor and premium amenities. Their breakfast, served in a garden setting, ranks among the island's finest. The hotel's shuttle service to nearby beaches adds considerable convenience.

Achladies - Peaceful Retreat

Panorama Hotel (Achladies Bay; +30 24270 48600) justifies its name with stunning views across the bay. Rooms starting at €140 all feature sea-view balconies. The infinity pool appears to merge with the horizon, creating perfect sunset photo opportunities. Their water taxi service to Skiathos Town adds convenience without sacrificing tranquility.

Practical Booking Advice

Peak season (July-August) demands booking at least six months ahead, especially for beachfront properties. Many hotels offer 15-20% discounts for early bookings made by January. Consider shoulder season (May-June or September) for better rates and availability while still enjoying excellent weather.

Most properties list rates in euros and require a deposit, typically 30% of the total stay. Cancellation policies vary significantly - carefully read terms before booking. Many family-run establishments prefer direct bookings and offer better rates than online travel agencies.

Regional Characteristics

- Skiathos Town properties often trade space for location. Expect smaller rooms but superior access to nightlife and restaurants. Light sleepers should request rooms away from bar areas, particularly during high season.

- Megali Ammos accommodations generally offer better value than Skiathos Town while maintaining easy access to urban amenities. Most properties here feature sea views and direct beach access.

- Troulos focuses on family comfort, with many accommodations offering kitchenettes and multiple rooms. The area's relative quiet makes it perfect for longer stays.

- Koukounaries properties emphasize their natural setting, with many incorporating extensive gardens and nature walks. The area's protected status limits development, maintaining exclusivity but reducing budget options.

- Achladies combines reasonable prices with peaceful surroundings. Properties here often include transportation solutions to compensate for the slightly removed location.

Service Variations by Price Point

- Luxury properties (€300+ per night) typically offer concierge services, room service, multiple dining options, and extensive spa facilities. Many provide airport transfers and excursion planning.

- Mid-range accommodations (€120-300) usually include breakfast, daily cleaning, and basic concierge services. Pool access becomes standard at this level, though beaches might require a short walk.

- Budget options (under €120) typically provide essential amenities - air conditioning, Wi-Fi, and basic cleaning services. Many offset limited facilities with exceptional locations or personal attention from owners.

- These accommodations reflect Skiathos's evolution from a simple island destination to a sophisticated resort haven while maintaining its authentic character. Whether seeking luxury isolation or immersion in local life, the perfect stay awaits - provided you plan adequately and book early enough to secure it.

Note: Rates mentioned reflect 2025 high season prices. Always verify current rates directly with properties as they may vary based on specific dates and availability.

2.4 Suggested Itineraries: From Weekend Breaks to Extended Stays

The art of experiencing Skiathos lies in matching your time constraints with the island's boundless offerings. Having explored this Aegean gem across different seasons and durations, I'll share carefully crafted itineraries that maximize every precious moment on the island.

48-Hour Whirlwind

Even a brief encounter with Skiathos can leave an indelible impression. Begin your first morning exploring Skiathos Town's narrow streets, starting at the old port as fishing boats return with their morning catch. Spend two hours wandering the cobblestone pathways, pausing at local bakeries for breakfast. By mid-morning, catch the water taxi to Koukounaries Beach, often celebrated as Greece's finest shoreline. The afternoon sun illuminates the crystal waters perfectly around 2 PM.

Your second day demands an early start. Book a morning boat tour (departing 9 AM) to Lalaria Beach, accessible only by sea. The white cliffs and electric-blue waters create otherworldly photo opportunities. Return by afternoon and dedicate your final hours to exploring the medieval castle ruins, timing your visit to catch the sunset over the Aegean around 7:30 PM.

5-Day Discovery

With five days, Skiathos reveals more of its secrets. Days one and two mirror the weekend break, but at a gentler pace. The third day invites exploration of the island's northern beaches. Rent a boat from the old port (book ahead in peak season) and discover secluded coves like Kechria Beach. The journey requires about 40 minutes each way, allowing ample time swimming in pristine waters.

Day four beckons cultural immersion. Visit the House of Alexandros Papadiamantis, opening at 10 AM. This preserved home of Greece's celebrated author provides fascinating insights into 19th-century island life. Afternoon cooking classes at Ergon Restaurant teach traditional recipes using local ingredients.

The final day combines hiking and beach time. The trail to Kastro (the old capital) takes roughly two hours, best started early to avoid midday heat. Descend to Kastro Beach afterward, where tavernas serve fresh catches for late lunch.

One-Week Immersion

A week allows deeper connection with island rhythms. Follow the five-day itinerary, then add these experiences. Day six introduces mountain biking through pine forests to hidden monasteries. Local operators provide guided tours leaving at 8 AM, returning mid-afternoon. Consider Evangelistria Monastery, dating from 1794, where monks still produce unique wines.

Day seven embraces water adventures. Morning scuba diving reveals underwater caves near Tsougria islet (book through Skiathos Diving Center). Afternoon wind-surfing lessons at Koukounaries Beach catch perfect afternoon breezes around 3 PM.

Two-Week Island Life

Extended stays permit themed daily adventures. Dedicate mornings to different activities: photography walks capturing dawn light on ancient walls, yoga sessions on quiet beaches, or bird watching in wetland sanctuaries. Afternoons might include cooking workshops, pottery classes, or sailing lessons.

Themed Experiences

Adventure Seekers: Combine daily water sports with hiking trails. The path to Kechria Beach offers rock climbing opportunities. Sea kayaking excursions reveal hidden caves along the northern coast. Mountain biking trails vary from beginner to advanced.

Cultural Immersion: Focus on traditional festivals (check local calendars), visit all 64 churches scattered across the island, and arrange meetings with local artisans. Evening music performances in Bourtzi showcase traditional instruments.

Family Fun: Banana boat rides at Megali Ammos Beach excite younger children. The Skiathos Dog Shelter welcomes families wanting to walk rescue dogs. Evening outdoor cinema screenings under stars create magical memories.

Relaxation Focus: Begin days with beach yoga, followed by spa treatments at luxury hotels (many accept outside guests). Afternoon meditation sessions in olive groves precede sunset watching from different vantage points.

Seasonal Considerations

Spring (April-May) brings wildflowers and mild temperatures perfect for hiking. Summer demands early starts to beat crowds and heat. Autumn offers warm seas and fewer tourists. Winter brings dramatic waves and cozy taverna evenings.

Greek time flows differently. Build flexibility into schedules, allowing spontaneous discoveries. Transportation between sites rarely exceeds 30 minutes, but summer traffic might require adjustment. Most importantly, embrace the unexpected - often creating the most cherished memories.

2.5 Travel Insurance and Health Considerations

During my extensive travels through the Greek islands, I've witnessed firsthand how crucial proper insurance and health preparation become when visiting Skiathos. The island's medical infrastructure, while adequate for common ailments, presents unique challenges that demand careful consideration.

Travel Insurance Essentials

Securing comprehensive travel insurance becomes vital when visiting Skiathos. The minimum coverage required by Greek authorities stands at €30,000 for medical expenses - a baseline requirement rather than an optimal amount. I recommend securing coverage of at least €50,000, especially if engaging in water sports or hiking activities.

Several insurance providers specialize in Greek island coverage. World Nomads and Allianz offer policies specifically designed for Mediterranean travel, including crucial provisions like helicopter evacuation. AXA's Mediterranean Plus policy particularly impresses me with its comprehensive coverage of water-related activities - essential given Skiathos's beach-centric attractions.

Key policy elements should include:
- Medical expenses coverage (minimum €50,000)
- Emergency evacuation (minimum €100,000)

- Personal liability protection (minimum €1,000,000)
- Coverage for adventure activities
- Trip cancellation and interruption
- Baggage loss and delay protection

Medical Facilities on Skiathos

The Skiathos Health Center (Papadiamanti Street; Emergency: +30 24270 22222) serves as the island's primary medical facility. Operating 24/7, it handles common medical issues effectively. The facility maintains an emergency room, basic diagnostic equipment, and a small pharmacy. However, complex cases typically require transfer to larger hospitals in Volos or Athens.

Several private medical clinics supplement the public health center:

- Skiathos Medical Practice (Harbor Area; +30 24270 21110) - English-speaking doctors, appointment required
- Aegean Clinic (Old Town; +30 24270 21666) - Specialized in tourist care, walk-ins accepted
- International Medical Center (Megali Ammos; +30 24270 24440) - Modern facilities, multilingual staff

Common Health Concerns

Summer heat poses significant risks. Dehydration affects numerous visitors annually, particularly during July and August when temperatures frequently exceed 35°C (95°F). The intense Mediterranean sun demands consistent sun protection - I've seen countless holidays ruined by severe sunburn.

Sea urchins inhabit rocky areas around beaches. While not dangerous, their spines cause painful injuries requiring proper medical attention. Always wear water shoes when exploring rocky shorelines.

Food-related illness, while uncommon, occasionally occurs. Stick to bottled water and exercise caution with street food during peak summer heat.

Preventive Measures

Vaccinations: Beyond routine immunizations, consider hepatitis A and B vaccines. While Greece poses minimal disease risks, these vaccines provide important protection when traveling.

Sun Protection: The Mediterranean sun intensifies between 11 AM and 4 PM. Use minimum SPF 30 sunscreen, reapplying every two hours. Wide-brimmed hats and UV-protective clothing prove invaluable.

Water Safety: Drink bottled water exclusively. While tap water meets EU standards, its mineral content might upset sensitive stomachs.

Emergency Procedures

In medical emergencies, dial 112 (EU-wide emergency number) or contact the Health Center directly. Staff typically speak basic English, but having a Greek-speaking person assist proves helpful.

For serious conditions requiring evacuation, three options exist:

- Helicopter transfer to Athens (2 hours)
- Speed boat transfer to Volos (1 hour)
- Ferry transfer to Volos (2.5 hours)

Insurance providers typically coordinate evacuations through their assistance centers. Keep insurance contact numbers readily available - I recommend storing them in your phone and carrying a physical copy.

Prescription Medications

Bring sufficient prescription medications plus extras. While pharmacies stock common medicines, specific prescriptions might prove difficult to obtain. Carry medications in original containers with prescriptions copies.

The main pharmacy (Central Square; +30 24270 22202) opens daily, with emergency service available after hours. Most pharmacists speak English and can offer basic medical advice.

Mental Health Support

Mental health services remain limited on Skiathos. The International Medical Center offers basic counseling services, but serious issues require treatment in larger cities. Ensure your insurance covers mental health support if needed.

Ultimately, while Skiathos provides adequate medical care for common issues, preparation remains essential. I've learned through experience that comprehensive insurance coverage brings peace of mind, allowing full enjoyment of this magnificent island's offerings. Remember, medical emergencies abroad can quickly become expensive - proper insurance represents a small investment protecting against potentially significant costs.

Chapter 3: Discovering Skiathos Town

3.1 Navigating the Old Town's Architecture

The architectural heritage of Skiathos Town unfolds like chapters in a living history book. Walking these streets, I've discovered how each stone and timber tells stories spanning centuries of Aegean life. Let me guide you through this remarkable open-air museum of traditional island architecture.

Begin your architectural exploration at the old port (Palio Limani), where fishing boats still bob against weathered stone quays. The port's protective seawall, built in 1906, marks the transition between maritime utility and urban charm. The district immediately behind the port showcases the quintessential Skiathian architectural style - two-story houses with stone foundations and wooden upper floors, a practical response to both earthquakes and summer heat.

Moving up Papadiamantis Street (the main thoroughfare), notice how buildings transition from maritime commercial to residential designs. At number 12, pause at the Kentrou House, an impeccably preserved example of 19th-century merchant architecture. Its iron balconies and blue-painted wooden shutters demonstrate the Turkish influences that shaped island design during Ottoman rule. The building's ground floor, once a merchant's store, retains its original broad arched doorway.

Turn right onto Polytechniou Street, where the residential architecture becomes more intimate. Traditional Skiathian homes here follow a consistent pattern: thick stone walls at ground level support wooden upper stories that often project slightly over the street. This design, known locally as "xeheilos" (overhanging), created additional living space while providing shade to the narrow streets below. The house at Polytechniou 8 exemplifies this style perfectly, its restored wooden balcony showcasing the intricate carpentry that characterized 19th-century craftsmanship.

The architectural walking route continues uphill along Evangelistrias Street, where you'll encounter the remarkable Church of Three Hierarchs (Treis Ierarches). Built in 1846, the church demonstrates how Skiathian builders adapted Byzantine architectural principles to local materials and techniques. The church's distinctive bell tower, added in 1901, combines Venetian and Orthodox design elements.

As you ascend, the streets narrow and buildings crowd closer together. This intentional urban planning provided protection from pirates and summer sun alike. The houses along these upper streets reveal another architectural innovation - the "sala," an upper-floor living room with windows on three sides, designed to catch sea breezes during sweltering summer months.

Preservation efforts concentrate heavily in this upper district. The Municipality of Skiathos maintains strict building codes ensuring renovations respect traditional methods and materials. Modern amenities must be carefully integrated behind historic facades. The Preservation Society of Skiathos (headquartered at Evangelistrias 45) offers excellent guided tours by appointment.

Following Agiou Nikolaou Street eastward brings you to the Bourtzi peninsula, where medieval fortress foundations support later Venetian military architecture. The Cultural Center here occupies a restored 13th-century structure, demonstrating how thoughtful renovation can adapt historic buildings to contemporary use while preserving their character.

Estimated walking times between key points:
- Old Port to Kentrou House: 5 minutes
- Kentrou House to Three Hierarchs Church: 12 minutes
- Church to Bourtzi: 15 minutes
- Complete circuit: 45-60 minutes at a leisurely pace

Accessibility varies significantly. While Papadiamantis Street offers relatively level walking, the upper town's steep, narrow streets and occasional steps present challenges. Summer heat makes morning or late afternoon walks advisable.

The evolution of Skiathian urban planning reflects centuries of adaptation to environmental and social pressures. The dense clustering of houses, strategic use of shade, and emphasis on natural ventilation all emerged from practical necessity. Today, these same features contribute to the town's environmental sustainability.

Notable architectural details to observe include:
- Wooden balconies supported by carved brackets
- Stone rain spouts (gargoyles) often decorated with marine motifs
- Traditional slate roofs laid in overlapping patterns
- Decorative door lintels indicating construction dates
- Corner supports ("gonies") made from dressed limestone

Understanding Skiathos Town's architecture enriches every subsequent walk through its streets. Each building becomes not just a structure but a testament to centuries of island life, adaptation, and artistic expression. As development pressures mount, appreciating this architectural heritage becomes ever more crucial to its preservation

3.2 The Port Area and Waterfront Experience

The heartbeat of Skiathos pulses strongest along its port, where centuries of maritime tradition blend seamlessly with modern coastal life. I've watched this harbor transform across seasons and years, each hour bringing its own distinct rhythm and character to the waterfront stretches.

Dawn breaks over the old fishing harbor (Palio Limani, northeastern end), where weathered wooden caïques head out as their ancestors have done for generations. By 6 AM, the first catches arrive, transforming the stone quay into an impromptu fish market. Local restaurateurs gather here, selecting the day's specialties directly from weather-worn crates while elderly fishermen mend their nets, sharing stories in low voices.

The commercial port section (Central Port, +30 24270 22017) handles ferry traffic with clockwork precision. Early morning brings island-hopping services to Skopelos and Alonissos, while afternoon ferries connect to mainland Volos and Thessaloniki. The port authority office, housed in a restored 1930s building, coordinates vessel movements with remarkable efficiency despite the summer crush.

Modern marina facilities occupy the western harbor (New Marina, +30 24270 21101), where gleaming yachts contrast sharply with traditional fishing vessels. Full-service berths accommodate boats up to 40 meters, offering electricity, water, and waste disposal. The marina's chandlery stocks essential supplies, while professional mechanics remain on call. Daily berthing rates range from €50 for smaller vessels to €200 for luxury yachts during peak season.

The waterfront's character shifts dramatically throughout the day. Morning's practical bustle gives way to afternoon promenading along the wide quayside walkway. This stretch between old and new harbors exemplifies thoughtful urban planning, balancing maritime operations with public enjoyment. Benches positioned at strategic intervals invite contemplation of harbor life, while shade trees offer respite from summer sun.

Dining options mirror this evolution from working port to sophisticated destination. En Plo (Old Harbor, +30 24270 21207) opens early, serving fishermen's breakfast - strong Greek coffee and fresh cheese pies. Their outdoor tables offer prime views of morning port activities. Midday brings crowds to Amfiliki (Central Port, +30 24270 22839), where grilled octopus and local wine complement harbor watching.

Evening transforms the waterfront again. Sunset cocktails at The Port Bar (Western Marina, +30 24270 21567) accompany spectacular views across moored yachts to painted skies. The harbor lights create shimmering reflections, while taverna music mingles with gentle wave sounds. Restaurant 1901 (Old Port, +30 24270 21901) serves refined Greek cuisine on a candlelit terrace overlooking illuminated fishing boats.

What distinguishes Skiathos's port from its Aegean neighbors? First, its natural protection - surrounding hills shelter vessels from prevailing winds, making it one of the safest natural harbors in the Sporades. Second, its seamless integration of commercial and leisure activities preserves authentic maritime culture while embracing modern tourism.

The waterfront's social geography reveals itself through careful observation. Fishermen gather at Kafeneion Olympia (Old Harbor, +30 24270 21344), discussing weather and catches over ouzo. Yacht crews frequent Marina Café (New Marina, +30 24270 21890) exchanging sailing tips and weather updates. Local families claim early evening spaces along the central promenade, while visitors fill waterfront bars as night falls.

Port services cater to every maritime need. Skiathos Boats & Motors (Western Harbor, +30 24270 21567) handles repairs and maintenance. The port authority coordinates daily water taxi services to nearby beaches (€10-15 round trip). A dedicated cruise ship tender pier efficiently processes thousands of visitors during peak season without disrupting regular port operations.

Best viewing spots change with the day's rhythm. Early risers should position themselves near the fish market steps for authentic port life. Midday boat-watching proves best from elevated café terraces along the central waterfront. Sunset photographers gather at the western marina's outer breakwater, where unobstructed views capture the interplay of light on water and vessels.

This vibrant waterfront stands as testament to Skiathos's ability to embrace change while honoring maritime heritage. Here, traditional fishing boats and superyachts share the same sheltered waters, each contributing to the port's unique character. As evening settles over the harbor, the blend of voices, music, and gentle wave sounds creates an atmosphere unique to this special corner of the Aegean.

3.3 Shopping Districts and Local Markets

The soul of Skiathos reveals itself through its markets and shops, where ancient trading traditions mingle with contemporary retail. My countless wanderings through these commercial arteries have unveiled layers of local culture expressed through crafts, foods, and daily commerce.

Papadiamantis Street forms the main shopping spine, its marble-paved length hosting an eclectic mix of establishments. Morning light catches the brass fixtures of Skiathos Gold (Papadiamantis 23; +30 24270 21456), where master goldsmith Dimitris Stavrou crafts jewelry incorporating ancient Sporades motifs. His signature pieces feature delicate filigree work inspired by local maritime traditions, with prices ranging from €50 for silver earrings to several thousand for elaborate gold necklaces.

The Traditional Market occupies the historic market hall (Central Square; +30 24270 21789), operating Monday through Saturday from 7 AM to 2 PM. Here, island producers display seasonal bounty - fat purple figs in late summer, pungent wild herbs year-round, and locally produced honey flavored by pine and thyme. The market's north corner houses dairy vendors offering fresh mizithra cheese and thick yogurt still made in mountain villages.

Authentic local products deserve special attention. The Skiathos Bee Museum and Shop (Evangelistrias 45; +30 24270 21435) showcases the island's renowned pine honey. Owner Maria Economou maintains traditional beekeeping practices, producing limited quantities of this distinctively flavored honey (€12-15 per jar). Her small museum section illuminates centuries-old honey-gathering techniques.

Along the narrower streets branching from Papadiamantis, artisan workshops maintain traditional crafts. Michalis Woodwork (Polytechniou 12; +30 24270 21234) continues three generations of expertise crafting olive wood items. Their workshop, fragrant with wood shavings, produces everything from practical kitchen implements (€15-40) to decorative pieces (€50-200). Each item comes with certification of sustainable wood sourcing.

The Textile Cooperative (Agiou Nikolaou 8; +30 24270 22567) preserves traditional weaving patterns. Eight local women work antique looms producing table linens, throws, and clothing incorporating designs documented in 19th-century island homes. Prices reflect countless hours of handwork - table runners start at €75, while elaborate bedspreads may reach €500.

Contemporary boutiques cluster along the waterfront. Archipelagos (Harbor Front 34; +30 24270 21678) curates designer resort wear with an emphasis on Greek designers. Nearby, Meltemi (Harbor Front 28; +30 24270 21345) specializes in locally designed jewelry incorporating sea glass and ceramic elements.

Market days transform quiet squares into bustling bazaars. Thursday brings traveling vendors to Church Square, selling everything from household goods to clothing. Sunday's Farmers' Market (7 AM-1 PM, Municipal Parking Area) draws producers from across the island. Negotiation remains part of market culture - a polite inquiry about "better price" often yields 10-15% reductions, particularly near closing time.

Notable artisans include ceramicist Anna Theologou (Studio at Plakes 15; +30 24270 21890), whose distinctive blue and white pieces reinterpret traditional patterns. Her workshop welcomes visitors (10 AM-2 PM, Monday-Friday), offering insights into her creative process. Prices range from €20 for small pieces to €200 for major works.

Operating hours follow traditional patterns - shops open 9 AM-2 PM, close for afternoon rest, then reopen 5:30 PM-9 PM (later in summer). Many smaller shops close Wednesday afternoons and Sundays. However, tourist-oriented businesses along the harbor front maintain longer hours during peak season.

The question of authenticity demands attention. True local crafts carry certification from the Skiathos Artisans Association. Mass-produced items masquerading as local work plague tourist areas - particularly concerning olive wood and textile products. Price often indicates authenticity - genuine handmade items reflect fair compensation for skilled labor.

Each shopping district maintains its distinct character. The old market area emphasizes traditional goods and foods. The harbor front caters to contemporary tastes. Side streets house specialist artisans and unexpected treasures. Together, they create a retail landscape where every purchase potentially connects buyer to centuries of island craft traditions.

3.4 Cultural Landmarks and Museums

The cultural institutions of Skiathos preserve stories spanning millennia, each building and collection adding depth to the island's rich narrative. Through years of visiting these spaces, I've watched them evolve from simple repositories into dynamic centers of living history.

The House of Alexandros Papadiamantis (Papadiamantis Street 12; +30 24270 22240) stands as the spiritual heart of Skiathian culture. This modest two-story structure, where Greece's celebrated author lived and wrote until 1911, perfectly preserves the ambiance of a 19th-century island home. Entry costs €4, with guided tours available hourly between 9:30 AM and 2:30 PM. The writer's spartan bedroom remains exactly as he left it - his iron bed, wooden desk, and well-worn prayer corner telling intimate stories of literary creation.

Inside, personal belongings illuminate Papadiamantis's daily life. His manuscripts, written in kathairevousa (formal Greek), reveal meticulous corrections in faded ink. The ground floor exhibition space contextualizes his works through photographs, letters, and first editions. Summer evenings bring readings of his stories in Greek and English (Thursdays, 7 PM, €5), making his words echo through the rooms where they were conceived.

The Maritime Museum (Harbor Front 45; +30 24270 21100) chronicles Skiathos's seafaring heritage. Housed in a restored merchant's mansion, its collection spans ancient trading vessels to modern fishing craft. Adult admission is €6, children under 12 enter free. The ground floor showcases ship models crafted with extraordinary precision, while the upper levels display navigation instruments, maritime documents, and dramatic photographs of island shipping through ages.

Special exhibits rotate quarterly - current displays examine traditional boatbuilding techniques (until September 2025). The museum's research library (open to scholars by appointment) contains valuable archives of shipping records and sailors' personal accounts. Monthly lectures (first Tuesday, 6 PM) feature maritime historians and retired sea captains sharing insights into island seafaring traditions.

Bourtzi Cultural Center (Bourtzi Peninsula; +30 24270 21511) occupies a Venetian fortress site, its restored buildings hosting exhibitions and performances. Entry varies by event, with many outdoor performances free to public. The permanent exhibition traces the peninsula's evolution from military stronghold to cultural hub through archaeological finds and architectural models. Summer brings outdoor theater performances in the ancient tradition, while winter focuses on intimate concert series in the converted powder magazine.

The Monastery of Evangelistria (3km north of town; +30 24270 21001) transcends simple religious significance as a museum of island resistance and resilience. This 18th-century complex, reached by hourly bus service (€2 each way), played crucial roles in Greece's independence struggle. Entry costs €5, including access to the monastery's museum of religious artifacts. The monastery's wine press still produces small quantities of traditional wine, while its library preserves rare manuscripts and early printed books.

Skiathos's Cultural Center (Town Hall Square; +30 24270 21816) serves as a hub linking these institutions. Its research facilities aid scholars studying island history, while its exhibition spaces showcase contemporary artists interpreting traditional themes. Free admission encourages regular visits from residents and tourists alike. The center coordinates cultural events across venues, including the popular Summer Festival of Arts (July-August).

Modern technology enhances visitor experiences throughout these institutions. The Maritime Museum's interactive displays allow virtual exploration of historic vessels. Papadiamantis House offers audio guides in eight languages (€3 rental). The Cultural Center's digital archives provide unprecedented access to historical photographs and documents.

These institutions actively preserve living traditions alongside historical artifacts. The Maritime Museum maintains workshops teaching traditional rope-making and knot-tying (Saturdays, 11 AM, €10). Evangelistria Monastery continues centuries-old practices of icon painting and manuscript conservation. The Cultural Center runs classes in traditional music and dance year-round.

Special access programs enhance engagement opportunities. Early morning visits to Papadiamantis House (Tuesday/Thursday, 8 AM, reservation required) allow intimate exploration before regular opening hours. The

Maritime Museum's "Behind the Scenes" tours (last Sunday monthly, €15) reveal conservation work and stored collections. School programs across all institutions ensure younger generations connect with their heritage.

Together, these cultural landmarks weave a complex portrait of island identity. Through careful preservation and dynamic programming, they maintain vital connections between past and present, ensuring Skiathos's rich cultural heritage remains vibrantly alive.

3.5 Evening Entertainment and Nightlife Spots

As evening descends on Skiathos Town, the streets pulse with an energy uniquely blending traditional Greek nightlife and contemporary entertainment. I've watched these venues evolve through changing seasons, each offering distinct flavors of island nightlife.

The Old Port district transforms as sunset paints the harbor. Ammos Music Bar (Old Port 23; +30 24270 21567) epitomizes sophisticated evening entertainment. Their outdoor terrace, adorned with vintage maritime artifacts, fills by 8 PM with both locals and visitors savoring craft cocktails. The resident mixologist, Andreas, crafts signature drinks incorporating local herbs and fruits. Try his mastiha-based "Aegean Sunset" (€12) while watching boats return in golden light.

Traditional music echoes from Alexandros Taverna (Market Street 12; +30 24270 21234), where weekly rebetiko performances recall Greece's rich musical heritage. Musicians gather Thursdays through Sundays from 9 PM, playing emotional songs on bouzouki and baglamas. The intimate space, seating only 40 guests, demands advance reservations during summer months. Cover charge includes mezedes (small plates) and house wine (€25 per person).

The cultural heart beats strongly at Bourtzi Open-Air Theater (Bourtzi Peninsula; +30 24270 21890), where summer evenings feature performances ranging from ancient Greek drama to contemporary dance. The 2025 season highlights include local interpretations of classic plays and visiting artists from Athens. Performances begin at 9 PM, with tickets ranging from €15-30. The venue's natural acoustics and harbor backdrop create unforgettable theatrical experiences.

Modern nightlife clusters along Bar Street (officially Polytechniou Street), where venues cater to varied tastes. Pure Club (Bar Street 34; +30 24270 21456) draws younger crowds with international DJs spinning from 11 PM until sunrise. The multi-level space features different music zones - electronic beats upstairs, mainstream hits at ground level. Entry costs €10, including first drink.

BBC Bar (Harbor Front 45; +30 24270 21789) represents Skiathos's cosmopolitan side. Their extensive cocktail menu and premium spirits selection attract sophisticated patrons. Live jazz performances (Wednesday/Saturday, 9 PM-midnight) showcase both Greek and international musicians.

The waterfront location offers perfect sunset viewing, though prices reflect the premium setting (cocktails €12-18).

Family entertainment thrives at Plakes Square, where seasonal events bring multi-generational appeal. The summer puppet theater (nightly except Monday, 7:30 PM) presents traditional Karagiozis shadow plays, delighting children and adults alike. Nearby, Paradise Ice Cream Parlour (Plakes 8; +30 24270 21345) stays open late, serving house-made gelato with harbor views.

Seasonal variations dramatically affect nightlife patterns. Summer sees venues operating at full capacity, with peak activity between 10 PM and 3 AM. Winter brings more intimate experiences, as establishments adjust to local patronage. Many venues close entirely November through March, though traditional tavernas maintain year-round operation with adjusted hours.

Rock Bar Skiathos (Market Street 78; +30 24270 21901) breaks the typical Greek island mold with live rock performances and an extensive beer selection. Their rooftop space offers aerial views of harbor activities while local bands perform Thursday through Sunday (10 PM-1 AM). The craft beer menu features Greek microbreweries alongside international selections.

Cultural performances extend beyond traditional venues. The Maritime Museum (Harbor Front 45) hosts evening events combining historical presentations with wine tasting and music. Their "Stories of the Sea" series (monthly, €20) pairs maritime tales with appropriate wines and traditional songs.

Sky Bar (Papadiamantis 56; +30 24270 21567) crowns a converted merchants house, offering panoramic views across tiled roofs to the harbor. Their signature event, "Full Moon Jazz" (monthly, weather permitting), combines live music with astronomical observation through provided telescopes. Advanced booking essential (€30, including two drinks).

Local regulations require most venues to moderate volume levels after midnight, though enforcement varies by season and location. Late-night food options cluster near bar areas - try Jimmy's Souvlaki Stand (Bar Street 12; open until 4 AM) offering authentic Greek street food.

Skiathos's nightlife distinguishes itself through this balanced blend of cultural richness and contemporary entertainment. Unlike many Greek islands focused solely on mainstream tourism, Skiathos maintains authentic entertainment traditions while embracing modern trends. The result creates memorable evenings whether seeking traditional Greek music, sophisticated cocktails, or dancing until dawn.

Chapter 4: Beaches and Coastal Adventures

4.1 Mapping the Golden Coastline

The beaches of Skiathos string along its coastline like precious gems, each shaped by unique geological forces over millennia. Having explored every cove and inlet, I'll share the distinct character of each stretch of shoreline, ensuring you find your perfect match.

Southern Coast - The Accessible Beauties

Megali Ammos emerges just a kilometer east of Skiathos Town. Reachable by a pleasant 15-minute walk along the coastal road or via hourly bus service (Bus Stop 2, €2), this golden stretch offers a gentle introduction to island beaches. The shore slopes gradually into crystal waters, while consistent afternoon breezes attract windsurfers. Two parking areas bookend the beach - the eastern lot (50 spaces, free) proves less crowded. Beach facilities include umbrella rentals (€10/day), four tavernas, and water sports rentals.

Vasilias Beach connects to Megali Ammos via a scenic coastal path (20-minute walk). This smaller cove, reached by bus (Stop 3) or car (limited roadside parking), provides a quieter alternative. Pine trees extend nearly to the water's edge, offering natural shade. Basic facilities include one beach cantina and umbrella rentals during peak season.

Moving eastward, Achladies Beach demonstrates how geography shapes visitor experience. High cliffs shelter this bay from winds, creating perfect swimming conditions. Access options include water taxi from Skiathos Town (€5 each way, running every 30 minutes), bus service (Stop 4), or car (organized parking, €5/day). Full facilities encompass restaurants, water sports centers, and beach chair rentals.

Southwestern Coast - The Famous Stretches

Koukounaries Beach occupies the island's southwestern tip, its perfect crescent shape created by centuries of wave action. Bus service (terminus at Stop 23) makes hourly runs from town (€4). The large parking area (200 spaces, €8/day) fills by mid-morning in peak season. A wooden boardwalk protects the rare cedar forest backing the beach. Complete facilities include water sports centers, restaurants, medical station, and accessibility ramps.

Maratha Beach, connected to Koukounaries by a five-minute woodland trail, offers similar golden sand with fewer crowds. No direct road access exists - reach it via the trail or water taxi from Koukounaries (€3). Limited facilities include one beach bar and umbrella rentals.

Northern Coast - The Hidden Treasures

Lalaria Beach stands as Skiathos's geological masterpiece, accessible only by boat. White cliff walls rise dramatically behind blindingly white pebbles, shaped smooth by endless waves. Morning tours depart from Skiathos Town harbor (€25, including 3-hour stay). No facilities exist - bring water and supplies. Swimming conditions vary with wind direction; check local forecasts.

Kastro Beach, below the ancient city ruins, rewards adventurous travelers. Access requires either a challenging 45-minute hike from the nearest road or boat service from Skiathos Town (€30 round trip, including guided history talk). The small pebble beach offers no facilities but provides unforgettable swimming beneath historical walls.

Coastal Connections

A marked coastal path connects many southern beaches, though conditions vary seasonally. The stretch from Skiathos Town to Koukounaries (12 kilometers) can be walked in sections, with plenty of swimming stops. Key viewpoints include:

- Bourti's Rock (between Vasilias and Achladies) - perfect sunrise spot
- Tzaneria Point (above Tzaneria Beach) - panoramic bay views
- Banana Beach overlook - spectacular sunset location

Beach-Hopping Tips

The public bus system provides the most economical beach access. Purchase multi-ride cards (€20 for 10 rides) at the terminal. During peak season (July-August), early morning or late afternoon trips avoid crowded buses.

Water taxis offer flexible beach-hopping. The main service (Harbor Office; +30 24270 22017) runs scheduled routes, while private boats offer custom tours. Most boats cease operation during strong winds - always have a backup plan.

Northern beaches experience stronger winds and rougher seas than southern counterparts. When strong northerlies blow, head south for calmer waters. Conversely, southern beaches can become uncomfortably busy during peak season - consider northern alternatives on crowded days.

4.2 Signature Beaches: From Koukounaries to Lalaria

Each signature beach of Skiathos holds its own distinct personality, shaped by natural forces and human stewardship. My years exploring these shores have revealed their subtle moods and hidden charms, which change with each passing hour and season.

Koukounaries Beach stands as Skiathos's crown jewel, a perfect crescent of golden sand stretching nearly a kilometer beneath an ancient cedar forest. The unusual combination of fine quartz sand and sheltering pines creates optimal swimming conditions - gentle slopes into crystalline waters reaching 25°C by midsummer. Morning brings calm seas ideal for families, while afternoon winds excite windsurfers.

Located 12 kilometers from Skiathos Town, Koukounaries welcomes visitors via frequent bus service (terminus at Stop 23, €4 one-way) or taxi (€25). The beach earned Blue Flag status through strict environmental controls, including protected zones for rare cedar trees and seasonal nesting areas for loggerhead turtles. Beach facilities maintain high standards: shower blocks, changing rooms, and accessibility ramps serve diverse needs. Multiple water sports centers offer equipment rentals and instruction - Koukounaries Water Sports (+30 24270 49301) specializes in windsurfing lessons (€50/hour).

Lalaria Beach presents Skiathos's most dramatic coastal scenery. Massive white cliffs tower above perfectly smooth white pebbles, creating an otherworldly landscape accessible only by sea. Morning boat tours depart Skiathos Town harbor (€25-35), timing visits to catch optimal light on the cliff faces. Swimming here means experiencing exceptional water clarity - visibility often exceeds 30 meters, though strong currents demand respect.

The beach's pristine condition stems from strict protection - no facilities exist, and visitors must carry out all waste. The famous Tripia Petra (hollow rock) arch frames magnificent photos, especially during morning light. Water temperature runs slightly cooler than southern beaches, typically 22-24°C in peak season.

Big Banana Beach earned its playful name from its curved shape, but its character runs deeper. This south-facing stretch captures maximum sunshine while remaining partially sheltered from prevailing winds. The coarse golden sand creates firm footing for beach sports, making it popular with volleyball enthusiasts. Regular bus service (Stop 21, €3.80) provides easy access, while two parking areas (€5/day) accommodate drivers.

The beach divides naturally into two sections: the main stretch buzzes with music and activity, while Little Banana around the headland attracts a quieter crowd. Water sports options abound - Banana Beach Sports (+30 24270 49444) offers jet ski rentals (€60/hour) and parasailing (€50/person). Several beach bars serve the area, with Banana Beach Bar known for sunset cocktails.

Vromolimnos combines natural beauty with excellent facilities. The deep bay shelters swimmers from most winds, while fine sand creates perfect conditions for beach activities. Located 8 kilometers from town (Bus Stop 19, €3.50), this beach balances accessibility with atmosphere. The beach club here (+30 24270 49700) maintains premium sunbeds (€15/day) and runs a sophisticated restaurant specializing in fresh seafood.

Water quality here consistently ranks among Greece's finest, with extensive monitoring protecting the delicate ecosystem. Morning snorkeling reveals abundant marine life around the bay's rocky edges. The beach slopes gradually, making it particularly suitable for children and less confident swimmers.

Kanapitsa presents yet another facet of Skiathian coastal beauty. This smaller beach compensates for its size with perfect southern exposure and exceptional facilities. Water taxi service from Skiathos Town (€5 each way) adds charm to arrival. The beach's protected position creates ideal conditions for learning water sports - Kanapitsa Water Sports Center (+30 24270 49288) specializes in waterskiing instruction.

Comparing these beaches to other Mediterranean destinations reveals Skiathos's unique appeal. While some Greek islands offer similar water clarity, few combine such diverse coastal environments within easy reach. The island's strict environmental protections preserve natural beauty while maintaining high-quality facilities - a balance many destinations struggle to achieve.

Each beach rewards repeated visits at different times. Early morning brings calm waters and pristine sand patterns. Midday highlights the waters' remarkable colors. Sunset transforms each beach uniquely - Koukounaries glows golden, while Lalaria's cliffs blush pink. These signature beaches embody Skiathos's natural wealth, each offering distinct experiences while maintaining their unspoiled character.

4.3 Water Sports and Maritime Activities

The waters surrounding Skiathos invite endless maritime adventures, each activity revealing new perspectives on this Aegean paradise. Through years of sampling these oceanic pursuits, I've gained intimate knowledge of the island's water sports scene, from gentle paddling to high-adrenaline thrills.

Wind Sports Excellence

Koukounaries Water Sports Center (Koukounaries Beach; +30 24270 49301) specializes in windsurfing and kiteboarding. Morning sessions suit beginners when thermal winds remain gentle. Afternoon breezes, typically reaching 15-20 knots, challenge more experienced riders. Introductory windsurfing lessons (€50/hour) include equipment and basic technique instruction. Five-day courses (€220) progress through safety, board handling, and basic planning.

Kiteboarding demands more extensive training. The center's VDWS-certified instructors provide mandatory safety courses (€80) before allowing equipment rental. Full beginner packages (€350) span three days, covering kite control, water starts, and riding basics. Equipment rental (€60/day) requires proof of certification.

Powered Water Sports

Tzaneria Watersports (Tzaneria Beach; +30 24270 49288) excels in motorized activities. Their waterskiing instruction progresses from basic stance to advanced slalom techniques. Early morning sessions benefit from calm waters - book 8 AM slots during peak season. Fifteen-minute lessons (€40) include equipment and boat time. Package deals (5 sessions, €180) offer better value during extended stays.

Jet ski tours explore Skiathos's southern coastline. Mandatory safety briefings precede rental (€60/30 minutes). Two-hour guided excursions (€150) visit secluded coves unreachable by land. Age restrictions (minimum 16 years) and weather conditions affect availability. Advance booking essential during July-August.

Diving Adventures

Skiathos Diving Center (Port Area; +30 24270 21855) maintains PADI certification standards. The discovery course (€80) introduces diving basics in protected waters. Open Water certification (€420) requires four days, combining theory, pool training, and ocean dives. Equipment rental (€45/day) includes full gear sets.

Advanced divers explore multiple sites. The Tunnel Cave (12-18m depth) offers dramatic underwater topography. March-May brings exceptional visibility, often exceeding 30 meters. Night dives (€65) reveal different marine species, while underwater photography courses (€90) capture submarine memories.

Paddle Sports

Blue Buddha Kayaking (Achladies Beach; +30 24270 49444) specializes in guided explorations. Single kayaks (€15/hour, €40/day) and doubles (€25/hour, €60/day) include safety equipment. Guided coastal tours (€50/person) explore hidden beaches and rock formations. Sunset paddles (€60) offer unique island perspectives.

Stand-up paddleboarding suits early mornings when waters remain mirror-smooth. Instruction (€30/hour) covers balance, paddling technique, and safety. Board rental (€20/hour) includes basic instruction and safety equipment. Yoga SUP classes (€40) combine core workouts with peaceful water time.

Sailing Experiences

Skiathos Sailing (Marina; +30 24270 21481) offers varied maritime experiences. Three-hour taster sessions (€60) introduce basic sailing concepts. RYA certification courses span multiple days - Competent Crew certification (€650) provides comprehensive sailing foundations. Bareboat charter requires appropriate licensing and experience verification.

Small boat rental (under 30hp) requires no license. Half-day rental (€80) includes safety briefing and area orientation. Larger vessels demand licenses and experience documentation. High-season availability remains limited - book weeks ahead during peak months.

Seasonal Considerations

May-June brings optimal conditions many activities. Moderate temperatures and lighter crowds allow focused instruction. July-August sees peak demand and prices. September offers warm waters and reduced rates, though some operators begin limiting services.

Morning sessions typically provide calmer conditions suitable beginners. Afternoon winds benefit intermediate and advanced practitioners. Weather conditions affect activity availability - operators maintain strict safety standards regarding wind and wave conditions.

Safety Standards

Reputable operators maintain current insurance and certification. Equipment undergoes regular safety checks - verify maintenance logs before signing rental agreements. Emergency procedures include radio communication and rapid response protocols. Medical certificates may be required certain activities.

All operators provide mandatory safety briefings. Language barriers necessitate clear communication - many instructors speak multiple languages, but verify instruction availability your preferred language. Insurance coverage varies - verify personal coverage before booking high-risk activities.

Pricing patterns follow seasonal demands. Early booking often secures better rates, especially package deals. Many operators offer morning discounts and multiple-day packages. Student and group discounts might apply - inquire when booking.

4.4 Hidden Coves and Secluded Spots

Beyond Skiathos's famous beaches lie hidden treasures known mainly to locals and adventurous souls. Years of exploration have revealed these secluded spots, each offering unique rewards to those willing to venture off beaten paths.

Kechria Beach nestles in a remote northern cove, reached by a challenging 45-minute hike from the nearest road end (parking available at Kechria Monastery). The trail descends through fragrant pine forest, requiring sturdy shoes and careful attention to marked paths. Morning visits prove optimal, as afternoon sun intensifies the return climb. The small pebble beach, framed by dramatic limestone cliffs, offers exceptional snorkeling opportunities in crystalline waters.

Essential preparations include water (minimum 2 liters per person), sun protection, and basic first aid supplies. Mobile phone coverage proves spotty - inform someone of your plans before departing. The beach lacks facilities, embracing its natural state. Spring visits reward hikers with hillsides carpeted in wild orchids and other endemic flora.

Arkos Bay, accessible only by small boat, hides behind a rocky headland west of Tsougria Island. Local fishermen offer informal transport (€30 round trip, arranged at old port), though weather conditions affect availability. The bay's unique geological formations include underwater caves and natural arch formations, creating memorable photography opportunities during morning light.

Marine life thrives in these protected waters - bring snorkeling gear to observe numerous fish species in their natural habitat. Sea urchins inhabit rocky areas; water shoes prove essential. The bay's orientation shields it from prevailing winds, though sudden weather changes demand awareness of boat pickup times.

Small Asselinos Beach requires a 20-minute scramble down a partially marked trail from the main Asselinos Beach. The effort yields solitude even during peak season. The trail begins behind the last taverna on main Asselinos, marked by a weathered wooden sign. Early morning visits catch beautiful light on the rocks and avoid afternoon heat. Pack minimal supplies - the climb back challenges heavily loaded visitors.

The cove's unique rock formations create natural pools at low tide, perfect small children exploring marine life. Underwater photographers find excellent macro subjects these pools. Exercise caution during rough seas, as waves can sweep across rocks without warning.

Glisteri Cove rewards adventurous spirits with a pristine environment accessible via either boat charter or a demanding 90-minute hike from Kastro. The hiking route follows ancient paths used by castle inhabitants, offering spectacular coastal views. Start early (7 AM recommended) avoid midday heat. The trail requires good fitness and hiking experience - loose scree and exposed sections demand careful attention.

The cove's ecological significance stems from its pristine state and minimal human impact. Rare seabirds nest in surrounding cliffs; maintain respectful distances during breeding season (March-June). The crystal-clear waters host diverse marine life - consider bringing an underwater camera capture the experience.

Xerxi Beach, reached by a 30-minute boat ride from Skiathos Town (private charter required, approximately €100 round trip), offers perhaps the island's most pristine swimming environment. The small crescent of white sand contrasts dramatically with dark rocks and deep blue water. Morning visits catch the best light for photography, while afternoon sun illuminates underwater scenery.

Responsible enjoyment of these locations demands careful attention to environmental impact. Pack out all waste - these pristine spots lack collection facilities. Avoid disturbing wildlife or removing natural items. Flash photography near nesting sites disrupts natural behaviors; maintain reasonable distances from wildlife.

Essential safety considerations include:
- Weather monitoring before departure
- Appropriate footwear for rough terrain
- Sufficient water and basic provisions
- Basic first aid supplies
- Charged mobile phone (though coverage varies)
- Sun protection and hats
- Timing visits avoid temperature extremes

Photography opportunities peak during "golden hours" - early morning and late afternoon. Consider neutral density filters capture dramatic seascapes. Underwater photography proves rewarding but requires proper equipment protection from sand and salt.

These hidden gems remind us of nature's unspoiled beauty. Their preservation depends entirely on visitor responsibility - each person entering these spaces becomes their temporary guardian. The effort required reaching these spots ensures they remain pristine, rewarding conscious travelers with memories of Skiathos few others experience.

4.5 Beach Facilities and Accessibility Guide

The quality and availability of beach facilities across Skiathos reveal much about each location's character. My extensive visits to these shores have shown how thoughtful infrastructure can transform a beautiful beach into a truly accessible paradise.

Koukounaries Beach exemplifies premium facilities with careful attention to accessibility. The beach entrance features a wide wooden boardwalk extending from the parking area to the waterline, accommodating wheelchairs and strollers. Beach-friendly wheelchairs remain available through the main office (free, reservation required). Modern changing rooms include accessible facilities with roll-in showers and support rails.

The sunbed operation here runs with remarkable efficiency - 400 sets of premium loungers (€15/pair daily) spread across designated zones. Early arrival ensures prime positions, though reserved spaces accommodate mobility-impaired visitors regardless of timing. Six shower stations provide fresh water, while four changing cabanas offer privacy. The medical station (staffed 10 AM-6 PM) maintains direct ambulance access and basic emergency equipment.

Megali Ammos, closest to Skiathos Town, balances accessibility with natural beauty. Concrete paths connect the road to three beach entry points, though some sections steep enough to require assistance. Four tavernas along the beach maintain their own sunbed sections (€10-12/pair), each offering table service to loungers. Clean restroom facilities require small purchase or nominal fee (€1).

The beach's gradual slope into shallow water suits families with young children. Lifeguards monitor two stations during peak season (June-September, 10 AM-6 PM). Emergency response times average 8 minutes from Skiathos Town's medical center. Several vendors rent beach umbrellas (€5-7/day) separate from sunbed packages.

Vromolimnos Beach demonstrates how private management can enhance accessibility. The beach club maintains immaculate facilities including marble-floored changing rooms, hot water showers (€2), and pristine restrooms. Their premium sunbed service (€20/pair) includes padded loungers, tables, and drink service. A dedicated family section offers smaller chairs and shaded play areas.

Medical support here includes a trained first responder on staff and automated external defibrillator. The beach club restaurant maintains wheelchair-accessible tables with spectacular views. Special assistance golf carts transport mobility-impaired visitors from parking area to beachfront (free service).

Troulos Beach specializes in family-frien
shallow, protected bay features a de
swimming area with floating boundary ....
facilities include:

- Supervised children's play area with shade
- Baby changing stations in all restrooms
- Fresh water foot-washing stations
- Multiple snack bars offering child portions
- Clear signage marking safe swimming zones

Sunbed operations here (€12/pair) include special family groupings with extra shade. The medical station coordinates with the local pediatric service during peak season. Regular beach cleaning maintains safe, debris-free sand especially important small children.

Achladies Beach excels in dining infrastructure. Five beachfront tavernas maintain private sunbed sections, each offering full menu service to beach visitors. Facility standards include:

- Modern restrooms with changing tables
- Freshwater showers (free with taverna purchase)
- Wooden walkways between restaurant and beach
- Evening lighting safe twilight swimming
- Multiple water stations

The beach's central location ensures quick emergency response (average 12 minutes). Regular water quality testing exceeds EU standards, with results posted weekly.

Kanapitsa Beach demonstrates thoughtful design smaller space. Despite limited area, facilities include:

- Accessible restrooms with support rails
- Dedicated rescue craft mooring
- First aid station (high season only)
- Multiple fresh water stations
- Clear emergency evacuation routes

Smaller beaches across the island maintain basic facilities through local taverna operations. These typically include:

- Basic restroom access
- Limited sunbed rentals
- Fresh water availability
- Emergency contact information
- Basic first aid supplies

Facility standards generally correlate with beach accessibility - remote beaches require self-sufficiency. However, all monitored beaches maintain minimum safety standards including:

- Emergency contact procedures
- Basic first aid capabilities
- Water quality monitoring

- Waste management systems
- Clear evacuation routes

Beach facility maintenance peaks during June-September, with reduced services during shoulder seasons. Winter visits require complete self-sufficiency as most infrastructure closes. Emergency services remain available year-round through central dispatch, though response times increase during off-season.

Chapter 5: Natural Heritage and Outdoor Activities

5.1 The Pine Forest Ecosystem

Walking through Skiathos's pine forests awakens every sense - the sharp scent of resin hanging in the warm air, needles crackling underfoot, and dappled sunlight filtering through the dense canopy. These majestic Aleppo pines (Pinus halepensis) blanket nearly 60% of the island, creating one of Greece's most pristine forest ecosystems.

The forest's heart beats strongest in the island's northern reaches, where centuries-old pines rise from rich, reddish soil. Their twisted trunks tell stories of survival against fierce winter winds. This ancient woodland harbors an intricate community of life - from tiny orchids pushing through pine needle carpets to elusive pine martens ghosting between shadows.

Spring transforms these woods into living gardens. Wild cyclamen and rock roses paint the forest floor in splashes of pink and white. The air fills with the sweet perfume of wild herbs - oregano, thyme, and sage growing in sunny clearings. Rare species like the Skiathos crocus (Crocus sieberi) emerge briefly, found nowhere else on Earth.

The forest provides sanctuary for remarkable wildlife. Sharp-eyed observers might spot Hermann's tortoises basking on sun-warmed rocks or hear the distinctive call of Scops owls at dusk. The endangered Mediterranean monk seal occasionally appears along the forested coastline, while various bat species roost in the deeper woods.

These pine forests serve as the island's ecological backbone. Their extensive root systems prevent soil erosion on Skiathos's steep slopes, while their canopies moderate the local climate. The trees act as natural water reservoirs, capturing moisture from sea breezes and slowly releasing it during dry summers. This process sustains countless streams and supports the island's freshwater springs.

Local culture and economy intertwine deeply with these woodlands. Traditional resin collection, though less common now, still continues in some areas, producing the distinctive retsina wine. The honey from Skiathos's pine forests carries unique aromatic qualities, prized throughout Greece. Many islanders still gather wild mushrooms and herbs, passing down knowledge through generations.

However, these precious ecosystems face mounting challenges. Climate change brings increased risk of devastating forest fires, while tourism development pressures some forest edges. Recent summers have seen concerning pine beetle infestations in certain areas. The local forestry service works tirelessly to monitor these threats and maintain firebreaks throughout the woodland.

Conservation efforts focus on sustainable management and education. The Skiathos Forest Protection Society, established in 2015, leads guided walks and workshops about forest ecology. They've implemented an innovative mobile app helping visitors identify species and report environmental concerns. Local schools regularly participate in tree planting initiatives, ensuring future generations understand their forest heritage.

Responsible visitors can access these magnificent woodlands through well-marked trails. The main forest entrance lies 3 kilometers north of Skiathos Town (coordinates: 39.1747° N, 23.4877° E). The forestry office provides detailed maps and safety guidelines. Remember - these forests demand respect. Carry water, wear appropriate footwear, and never light fires. Take only photographs, leave only footprints.

The most accessible forest areas include the Mandraki Peninsula Trail, offering stunning coastal views through pine-framed vistas. The more challenging Kastro Forest Path winds through old-growth sections to medieval ruins. For serious hikers, the full-day Forest Ridge Trail reveals the island's most pristine woodland stretches.

Each forest area holds distinct features. The southeastern woods near Koukonaries showcase rare coastal pine formations, while the northwestern forest contains the island's oldest trees, some exceeding 300 years. Small wetland areas dot the central forest, creating vital diversity in the ecosystem.

Beyond their ecological significance, these forests shape Skiathos's identity. Their presence moderates summer temperatures, making the island more appealing to visitors. The distinctive pine-scented air has become synonymous with Skiathos holidays. Local architecture traditionally incorporates pine timber, while forest-inspired art fills island galleries.

The future of Skiathos's pine forests depends on balancing conservation with thoughtful access. Current initiatives include expanding protected areas, improving trail infrastructure, and developing sustainable forest-based activities like guided nature photography. The island's authorities increasingly recognize these woodlands as both natural treasure and economic asset.

Research continues to reveal new aspects of this ecosystem. Recent studies have identified previously unknown fungal species and documented the forests' role in carbon sequestration. This growing understanding helps inform protection strategies and underscores these woodlands' global significance.

Standing beneath these towering pines, feeling their ancient presence, reminds us why preserving such places matters. They represent nature's resilience, beauty, and ability to sustain life in countless forms. Skiathos's forests offer more than scenic beauty - they provide hope that with careful stewardship, such natural wonders can endure for future generations to experience and cherish.

5.2 Hiking Trails and Walking Routes

Skiathos reveals its soul through its network of walking paths, each trail whispering stories of ancient feet and timeless landscapes. These routes weave through the island's varied terrain, revealing hidden coves, hilltop monasteries, and breathtaking viewpoints that mere roads could never reach.

The Kastro Trail stands as the island's premier hiking experience. Beginning at the old harbor (37.8445° N, 23.4877° E), this moderate-to-challenging route climbs steadily through pine forests to reach the medieval fortress settlement. The 7.5-kilometer path demands approximately 4 hours round trip, with an elevation gain of 270 meters. Morning hikers catch sublime eastern views across the Aegean, while afternoon light bathes the western slopes in golden hues. Essential stops include the restored chapel of Agios Georgios and several Byzantine-era cisterns.

Equipment needs vary by season. Summer hiking requires sturdy walking shoes, sun protection, and at least 2 liters of water per person. Winter trails demand waterproof boots and layered clothing - the exposed ridges catch bitter north winds. Every hiker should carry a basic first aid kit, trail mix, and a fully charged mobile phone regardless of season.

The gentler Mandraki Peninsula Circuit suits less experienced walkers. This 5-kilometer loop from Skiathos Town takes roughly 2.5 hours, following well-marked coastal paths past secluded beaches. Spring hikers encounter carpets of wildflowers, while autumn brings perfect clarity to the dramatic sea views. Three designated rest stops provide shade and seating, with the halfway point offering access to a peaceful pebble beach.

More ambitious hikers embrace the challenging Ridge Route, connecting the island's highest points. Starting from Kechria Beach (reached by morning boat service or taxi), this 12-kilometer trail requires 6-7 hours and serious stamina. The 450-meter elevation gain rewards persistent climbers with panoramic views stretching to Mount Pelion and neighboring islands. Water sources exist at kilometers 4 and 8, but carrying adequate supplies remains essential.

Each trail showcases unique aspects of Skiathos's natural heritage. The Monastery Path reveals the island's spiritual history, linking three restored religious sites through olive groves and cypress stands. The Koukounaries Nature Trail highlights coastal ecosystems, with informative panels explaining the delicate wetland habitat. The remote Northern Circuit passes ancient agricultural terraces, telling stories of traditional island life.

Safety considerations demand respect. Summer hiking should begin early, avoiding the intense midday heat. Winter trails become treacherous after rain, particularly on marble-rich slopes. Emergency services maintain a 24-hour hotline (dial 112), with helicopter evacuation available if necessary. Local authorities strongly advise against solo hiking on remote trails.

Preparation makes the difference between pleasure and predicament. Download offline maps through the Skiathos Trails app, showing current position even without signal. Register your planned route at your accommodation. Pack appropriate gear: hiking poles help on steep sections, while a lightweight windbreaker protects against sudden weather changes.

The Dog's Head Peninsula Trail offers perhaps the island's most dramatic coastal walking. This 6-kilometer route (3.5 hours) requires scrambling across rocky sections, but delivers extraordinary views of wave-carved cliffs and hidden sea caves. Morning light creates perfect photography conditions, while late afternoon brings chances to spot seabirds returning to roost.

Seasonal considerations shape the hiking experience. Spring trails burst with orchids and cyclamen, but require careful footing on damp paths. Summer brings reliable weather but demands early starts and sun protection. Autumn offers perfect hiking temperatures and crystal-clear views. Winter walking reveals another island entirely - peaceful, mysterious, and occasionally challenging.

Trail maintenance relies on dedicated local volunteers. The Skiathos Hiking Club marks routes using international standards: red and white stripes for main paths, yellow for connecting trails. They also maintain emergency shelters at strategic points, equipped with basic supplies and radio links to town.

Beyond physical preparation, these trails demand mental engagement. Each path tells environmental and human stories - from the geological forces that shaped the island to the generations who worked this land. Taking time to read the landscape enriches every step.

Rest stops deserve careful planning. The Kalamaki Forest shelter provides a covered lunch spot with wonderful valley views. The restored shepherd's hut on the Ridge Route offers emergency overnight accommodation. Several trails pass traditional kafeneia in remote villages, where local hospitality refreshes tired hikers.

Every trail holds secrets waiting to be discovered. Dawn hikers might glimpse shy pine martens. Patient observers find rare orchids hiding beside paths. Storm-weathered rocks reveal fossil traces of ancient sea life. These paths offer more than exercise - they provide windows into Skiathos's soul.

5.3 Bird Watching and Wildlife Observation

Skiathos holds a remarkable position along Mediterranean migration routes, transforming the island into a living theater of wild encounters. Spring brings waves of raptors soaring on thermal currents, while autumn sees shorebirds probing tidal flats. Year-round residents add depth to this ecological performance, creating opportunities during every season.

The Koukounaries wetland complex stands as the island's premier wildlife observation site. Located at the northwestern edge (39.1486° N, 23.4031° E), this protected area encompasses freshwater pools, salt marsh, and dense reed beds. Dawn visits reward observers with hunting marsh harriers skimming the reeds, while purple herons stalk through shallow waters. The raised observation platform provides excellent views without disturbing wildlife.

Serious bird watching requires proper equipment. Binoculars with 8x42 or 10x42 magnification suit most situations, balancing power with field of view. A spotting scope proves invaluable at wetland sites, revealing distant waders and waterfowl. The "Birds of Greece" field guide helps identify unfamiliar species, while the Skiathos Bird Recording app enables instant logging of observations.

Spring migration peaks between March and May, bringing spectacular raptor movements. Honey buzzards pass in impressive numbers, joined by lesser spotted eagles and occasional Egyptian vultures. The cliffs near Kastro offer perfect vantage points, where patient observers might spot blue rock thrushes nesting among ancient walls. Early mornings provide optimal viewing conditions before sea breezes strengthen.

The island's various ecosystems support distinct wildlife communities. Pine forests harbor breeding short-toed treecreepers and coal tits, their calls echoing through resinous air. Olive groves attract Syrian woodpeckers and masked shrikes, while coastal scrub conceals sardinian warblers and subalpine warblers. Each habitat adds unique species to Skiathos's biological richness.

Ethical wildlife viewing demands respect and patience. Maintain safe distances using optical equipment rather than approaching animals. Avoid nesting areas during breeding season. Never bait or call wildlife - natural behavior provides the most rewarding observations. The local environmental organization provides guidance on responsible practices through their visitor center.

Summer brings different wildlife opportunities. Eleonora's falcons, elegant seasonal residents, hunt migrating birds over coastal headlands. These specialized raptors time their breeding to coincide with autumn bird migration, providing spectacular aerial displays. The morning boat trip around northern cliffs offers chances to observe their nesting colonies.

Conservation efforts focus on protecting critical habitats. The Koukounaries wetland earned international recognition under the Ramsar Convention, highlighting its importance for migratory birds. Local initiatives monitor breeding success of key species, while habitat restoration projects improve wildlife corridors between fragmented areas.

Notable resident species include long-legged buzzards, which maintain territories in the island's rugged interior. Their distinctive calls carry across valleys year-round. Careful observers might spot Hermann's tortoises in forest clearings or glass lizards sunning themselves on rocky slopes. Each creature plays a vital role in the island's ecological web.

Autumn migration stretches from late August through October. The Koukounaries lagoon attracts wading birds - wood sandpipers, little stints, and occasional rarities like broad-billed sandpipers. Evening visits offer chances to observe European nightjars hunting insects over the dunes. Keep detailed records of observations - they contribute to wider conservation research.

Winter brings its own wildlife spectacle. Northern birds seek Mediterranean warmth, bringing flocks of black-necked grebes to sheltered bays. Alpine swifts swoop around cliff faces, while wintering blue rock thrushes add color to stone walls. The reduced tourist presence creates perfect conditions for undisturbed observation.

Different locations require specific approaches. The pine forest trails demand quiet walking and frequent stops to detect movement. Wetland hides require patience and stillness. Coastal watching benefits from a stable position protected from wind. Understanding these basics improves observation success.

The island's marine life adds another dimension. Bottlenose dolphins regularly patrol the coast, while Mediterranean monk seals occasionally haul out on remote beaches. Dawn boat trips maximize chances of encountering these marine mammals, though maintaining appropriate distances remains crucial.

Conservation challenges persist. Development pressures threaten some wildlife habitats, while climate change alters traditional migration patterns. Local conservation groups work to address these issues through research, habitat protection, and public education. Their efforts ensure future generations might experience similar natural wealth.

Understanding wildlife behavior enhances observation opportunities. Many birds follow daily routines - morning feeding, midday rest, evening activity. Learning these patterns helps predict likely encounters. Local knowledge proves invaluable; consulting resident naturalists often reveals lesser-known observation sites.

5.4 Photography Locations and Viewpoints

Skiathos presents an endless canvas of photographic possibilities, where light plays across ancient stones and sea meets sky in dramatic collisions. Each location demands different approaches as the sun charts its course through Mediterranean skies.

Kastro's ruins command the northern headland, offering unparalleled dawn photography opportunities. Arriving 45 minutes before sunrise (coordinates: 39.2114° N, 23.4973° E) allows setup time in the blue hour. The first light strikes the eastern walls with intense warmth, creating stark contrasts against deep shadows. A wide-angle lens (16-35mm) captures the scale of fortress walls against the sea, while a medium telephoto (70-200mm) isolates architectural details illuminated by early rays.

Technical considerations at Kastro require careful attention. The exposed position brings strong winds - stabilize your tripod with a lower center of gravity and shield it with your body when necessary. Graduated neutral density filters help balance bright skies with darker foreground elements. Winter mornings often bring atmospheric mist rolling in from the sea, adding mood to historical compositions.

Lalaria Beach reveals its photographic magic during mid-morning hours. The iconic white arch and marble pebbles reflect light intensely - keeping highlights in check requires careful exposure compensation (-0.7 to -1.0 EV). Accessible only by boat, morning tours from the old port provide optimal arrival times. Underwater photographers discover exceptional clarity, with sunbeams penetrating sea caves between 10 AM and noon.

The Koukounaries wetland transforms through daily and seasonal cycles. Summer evenings bring golden light streaming through reed beds, while winter storms create moody reflections. A telephoto lens proves essential here - birds and wildlife appear more naturally when photographed from the dedicated hides. Experiment with slow shutter speeds (1/15 - 1/4 sec) to capture reed movement in gentle breezes.

Monastery Hill presents diverse compositions as daylight shifts. The whitewashed walls reflect changing colors of sky, while cypress trees create strong vertical elements. Late afternoon light rakes across the textured stone, revealing centuries of weathering. A circular polarizer reduces glare from foliage and enhances cloud detail. Spring visits catch wildflower carpets adding foreground interest.

Technical mastery elevates results at each location. The island's intense light demands careful metering - spot metering helps manage contrast in challenging situations. Keep ISO low (100-400) during golden hours to maximize dynamic range. Many scenes exceed normal exposure latitude - bracketing exposures enables HDR blending if needed.

Secret sunrise spots reward adventurous photographers. The ridge above Kechria Beach offers phenomenal views east toward Mount Pelion. Arrive early to catch pre-dawn colors reflecting off still waters. The rough track requires a headlamp and sturdy boots, but determined photographers find pristine conditions without footprints marring beach compositions.

Seasonal changes create distinct opportunities. Winter storms generate dramatic seascapes along the north coast - fast shutter speeds (1/1000 sec minimum) freeze explosive wave action. Spring brings ethereal morning mist to the valleys, while autumn clarity creates perfect conditions for long-range landscapes. Summer demands attention to harsh contrast - shoot during edge hours or use diffused light under pine canopies.

The Dog's Head Peninsula combines geological drama with perfect sunset alignment. The twisted rock strata tell ancient stories, while waves carved sea caves create natural frames. Time visits to catch the golden hour lighting cliff faces. A sturdy tripod helps in high winds, while neutral density filters enable longer exposures to smooth water movement.

Urban photography in Skiathos Town peaks during blue hour. The old port's lanterns create leading lines reflected in still morning waters. Traditional architecture demands vertical composition - shift lenses help maintain parallel lines when shooting upward. Dawn brings perfect light to narrow streets before crowds appear.

Advanced techniques unlock creative possibilities. Long exposures under full moons paint ethereal seascapes. Focus stacking captures sharp detail from foreground rocks through distant horizons. Time-lapse sequences record cloud movement across ancient sites. Each technique requires specific preparation and equipment.

Weather patterns influence shooting strategies. The north wind (meltemi) brings crystal clarity ideal for long-range shots but challenges stability. South winds often carry humidity, reducing contrast but adding atmospheric effects. Understanding local conditions helps plan productive sessions.

Conservation awareness shapes responsible photography. Maintain distance from nesting birds and wildlife. Avoid trampling sensitive vegetation getting "the shot." Many premier locations lie within protected areas - respect access guidelines and time restrictions. Small actions preserve these places for future photographers.

Professional gear preparation matters in this environment. Salt spray and dust demand regular sensor cleaning. Carry multiple batteries - summer heat increases power consumption. A rocket blower removes marble dust from lenses. Weather-sealed equipment provides confidence in changeable conditions.

5.5 Environmental Conservation Efforts

Skiathos stands at an environmental crossroads, where increasing tourism pressures clash with fragile Mediterranean ecosystems. Understanding these challenges reveals how visitors and residents alike shape the island's ecological future.

The Koukounaries wetland exemplifies both environmental threats and conservation successes. This vital ecosystem faces pressure from nearby development, yet dedicated efforts have preserved its core functions. The Skiathos Environmental Protection Society established a buffer zone in 2020, limiting construction within 500 meters of wetland boundaries. Scientific monitoring shows encouraging results - wading bird populations increased 23% since these protections began.

Marine conservation demands particular attention. The island's waters harbor endangered Mediterranean monk seals and critical seagrass meadows. Local fishermen now participate in a pioneering program, modifying fishing gear to reduce accidental catches while maintaining sustainable harvests. The "Sea Life Skiathos" initiative, launched in 2023, created underwater observation points where visitors learn about marine ecosystems without disturbing them.

Plastic pollution emerged as a critical challenge. Beach cleanup data revealed 70% of waste originated from tourist activities. In response, the municipality implemented an innovative reward system - visitors exchanging collected beach plastic receive discount vouchers at participating businesses. Local restaurants joined the effort, eliminating single-use plastics and offering reusable containers for takeaway meals.

Pine forest protection requires constant vigilance. Climate change increases fire risks, while beetle infestations threaten tree health. The Forestry Service expanded its monitoring network, installing early warning sensors throughout woodland areas. Visitors now access real-time forest health data through the "Skiathos Nature" app, reporting concerns directly to conservation teams.

Successful initiatives demonstrate effective conservation approaches. The "Save Our Seabirds" project established protected nesting areas along coastal cliffs, resulting in the first recorded Eleonora's falcon breeding success in a decade. Local schools adopted sections of coastline, combining education with hands-on conservation experience. These programs show how community involvement strengthens environmental protection.

Sustainable tourism practices make measurable differences. Hotels participating in the "Green Island" certification program reduced water consumption by 40% through efficient fixtures and guest education. Tour operators now limit group sizes at sensitive sites, while guided nature walks emphasize minimal impact principles. Visitors choosing certified providers directly support conservation through dedicated funding channels.

Habitat restoration projects transform damaged areas. The abandoned quarry near Kanapitsa metamorphosed into a biodiversity hub through careful replanting with native species. Beekeepers established traditional hives along restored areas, promoting pollinator populations while producing premium honey. Similar projects await support across the island.

Urban development poses ongoing challenges. The municipality adopted strict guidelines requiring environmental impact assessments for new construction. Building height restrictions preserve natural skylines, while mandatory green spaces maintain wildlife corridors through developed areas. Visitors witness these policies in action through living walls and rooftop gardens brightening town structures.

Scientific research underlies conservation strategies. The University of Thessaly maintains research stations monitoring climate change impacts on island ecosystems. Their findings guide adaptation strategies, from selecting drought-resistant plant varieties to identifying vulnerable species requiring additional protection. Visitors can attend weekly presentations sharing latest research developments.

Individual actions create collective impact. The "Conscious Traveler" program educates visitors about sustainable practices - using refillable water bottles, staying on marked trails, and properly disposing of waste. Local businesses offer incentives for eco-friendly choices, from discounted bike rentals to rewards for plastic-free shopping.

Traditional practices often align with conservation goals. Local farmers maintaining ancient olive groves preserve crucial habitat for native species. Traditional grazing patterns prevent woodland encroachment while supporting rare meadow plants. Connecting these heritage practices with modern conservation science creates resilient strategies for future protection.

Funding remains crucial for conservation success. The "Friends of Skiathos Nature" foundation channels donations into specific projects, providing transparent reporting on outcomes. Visitors purchase symbolic adoption certificates for endangered species, supporting monitoring and protection efforts. Local art galleries contribute through exhibitions highlighting environmental themes.

Looking ahead, Skiathos faces intensifying environmental pressures. Rising sea levels threaten coastal habitats, while changing weather patterns stress native species. Yet growing environmental awareness drives innovative solutions. New technologies support traditional conservation methods, while international cooperation brings additional expertise and resources.

Every visitor influences Skiathos's environmental future. Simple choices - reducing plastic use, respecting wildlife distances, supporting eco-certified businesses - ripple through island ecosystems. Understanding these connections transforms tourists from observers into active participants in preservation efforts. The island's natural heritage endures through this shared commitment to conservation.

Chapter 6: Culinary Journey

6.1 Traditional Skiathian Cuisine

The kitchens of Skiathos whisper stories passed down through generations, each recipe carrying the essence of island life shaped by sea winds and sun-baked soil. This distinct culinary heritage sets itself apart from mainland Greek traditions through unique preparations and ingredients born of necessity and innovation.

Amygdalota stands as Skiathos's signature sweet, yet locals prepare these almond cookies differently than other Greek islands. At Zaxaroplasteio Stamatis (Papadiamantis Street 12, +30 24270 22218), third-generation confectioners still use the original 1920s recipe. Their version incorporates orange blossom water and a touch of mastic, creating a more complex flavor profile. The shop opens daily from 8 AM to 10 PM, easily reached by a five-minute walk from the old port.

The island's demographic history profoundly influenced its cuisine. Refugees from Asia Minor brought sophisticated spice combinations in the 1920s, transforming local fish preparations. This fusion survives at Mourgia (Harbor Front 35, +30 24270 21400), where the kakavia fish soup sings with saffron and wild fennel. Morning visitors might catch owner Maria selecting fresh catch directly from returning boats.

Skiathian cheese pie diverges dramatically from typical Greek tyropita. Local bakers layer paper-thin phyllo with a mixture of aged myzithra and fresh herbs, then fold it into distinctive triangular shapes. The legendary Kyra Maria (Old Town Square 8, +30 24270 21605) still bakes these daily in wood-fired ovens, opening at 6 AM until supplies last. Her small shop sits tucked behind the cathedral, marked by blue doors and intoxicating aromas.

Seasonal rhythms dictate traditional cooking. Spring brings xynohontros, a unique fermented grain preparation originally developed by shepherds. Local women still gather wild greens like kritama and vlita, transforming them into complex braised dishes. The restaurant To Kali Kardia (Mountain Road 45, +30 24270 22980) maintains these seasonal traditions, adjusting its menu weekly based on available ingredients.

The humble chickpea receives royal treatment in Skiathos. Unlike typical Greek revithia, island cooks slow-roast the legumes with whole heads of garlic and bay leaves in sealed clay pots. This method, perfected over centuries, produces exceptionally creamy results. Experience this at O Simos (Plateia Trion Ierarchon 4, +30 24270 21521), where pots emerge from wood-fired ovens every Friday, drawing crowds of knowing locals.

Maritime influences permeate every aspect of Skiathian cuisine. Fishermen developed astakomankarado, a unique lobster preparation using sweet wine and bitter oranges to preserve their catch. Modern versions of this dish shine at Thessaloniki (Port Road 78, +30 24270 22790), where Chef Yannis maintains his grandfather's exact recipe, including the traditional three-day marination period.

Pine honey plays a crucial role in island sweets. Local beekeepers position hives specifically to capture pine forest essences, producing honey with distinctive resinous notes. This special ingredient elevates traditional desserts like karydopita at Glykopolio (Market Street 23, +30 24270 21890), where bakers incorporate century-old techniques into modern creations.

The island's isolation historically necessitated preservation methods that evolved into delicacies. Salt-cured fish, particularly kolios (mackerel), undergoes a unique smoking process using pine needles. The technique survives at Psarokokkalo (Fish Market 5, +30 24270 22456), where visitors can watch traditional smoking sessions every Tuesday and Friday morning.

Agricultural traditions shape distinctive vegetable preparations. Mountain settlers developed wrapped vine leaf dishes using wild grape leaves, stuffed with unique grain and herb combinations. These recipes endure at To Perivoli (Upper Town 67, +30 24270 21901), where grandmother and granddaughter still gather leaves from specific vineyard locations based on flavor profiles.

Family recipes guard the heart of Skiathian cuisine. The Moschovis family (Traditional Taverna, Church Square 12, +30 24270 21678) maintains their great-grandmother's spice mixture for stifado, incorporating unusual additions like allspice and wild sage. Their restaurant opens evenings only, requiring advance bookings during summer months.

Each village contributes unique specialties to the island's culinary mosaic. Kalyvia's bread makers still use chestnut flour in winter loaves, while Troulos maintains distinct preparations of octopus using local wine. Understanding these micro-regional differences reveals the depth of Skiathian gastronomy.

6.2 Restaurant Guide by Region

Skiathos Town Waterfront

Bakaliko Modern Kitchen stands as an innovative beacon along the old harbor (Harbor Front 23, +30 24270 21950). Chef Maria Nikolaou transforms traditional ingredients into contemporary masterpieces while maintaining authentic flavors. The sea bass carpaccio with citrus and mountain herbs exemplifies her approach. Reservations become essential three days ahead during peak season, especially for the coveted sunset tables. Dinner service runs 6 PM - 11 PM, with lunch served weekends only. A taxi from anywhere in Skiathos Town costs approximately €8.

Nearby, To Kochyli (Port Walk 45, +30 24270 21875) maintains time-honored seafood preparations in an atmospheric setting. Their octopus, slow-cooked in aged vinegar and bay leaves, draws devoted regulars every evening. The restaurant's blue-and-white interior mirrors the harbor views, while the outdoor terrace accommodates romantic dining under the stars. Open daily 12 PM - 12 AM, with fresh fish selections varying by morning catch. Walking distance from central bus stop.

Koukounaries Beach Area

Ambelakia Restaurant (Koukounaries Beach Road 12, +30 24270 49220) perfectly balances sophisticated cuisine with barefoot beach comfort. Their kitchen specializes in creative Mediterranean dishes using locally sourced ingredients. The zucchini fritters with sheep's milk yogurt sauce highlight regional produce. Summer evenings require bookings two weeks ahead. Bus route 14 stops directly outside. Open April-October, 11 AM - 11 PM.

Hidden behind pine trees, Kivos (Western Koukounaries Path 3, +30 24270 49445) offers an intimate dining experience focused on grilled specialties. Their lamb chops, seasoned with wild herbs gathered from nearby hills, achieve legendary status among returning visitors. Evening service includes live traditional music on Thursdays. Reservations recommended during high season. Accessible via 15-minute walk from Koukounaries bus terminus or €12 taxi ride.

Troulos Region

Infinity Blue (Troulos Bay Road 78, +30 24270 49780) elevates seaside dining through exceptional attention to detail. Panoramic windows frame spectacular sunsets while innovative dishes showcase local ingredients. Their sea urchin pasta changes daily based on availability. Open year-round, 12 PM - 12 AM, with winter hours varying. Advance bookings essential for sunset tables. Located 200 meters from Troulos bus stop.

Family-run Mama's Kitchen (Troulos Village Square, +30 24270 49565) maintains authentic home-style cooking traditions. Their moussaka recipe, unchanged since 1965, brings locals from across the island. The welcoming atmosphere encourages lingering over shared plates. No reservations accepted - arrive before 7 PM to secure a table. Ten-minute walk from Troulos beach, following signed path.

Kanapitsa Peninsula

Overlooking the yacht harbor, Blue Water (Marina Complex 5, +30 24270 49890) specializes in refined seafood preparations. Their lobster spaghetti requires 24-hour advance ordering but rewards patience with extraordinary flavor. The elegant interior features local artworks, while terrace dining offers marina views. Open 6 PM - 11 PM, closed Mondays. Water taxi service available from Skiathos Town.

The Olive Grove (Kanapitsa Hill 34, +30 24270 49670) creates magical evening atmospheres among centuries-old olive trees. Their slow-cooked lamb kleftiko emerges from traditional clay ovens every evening at 8 PM. Romantic lighting transforms the garden setting after sunset. Reservation essential - book through their website. Shuttle service available from major hotels.

Achladies Bay

Taverna Alexandros (Achladies Beach Road 56, +30 24270 49340) masters the art of simple, perfectly executed Greek classics. Their grilled fresh fish selection changes twice daily based on local catches. The beachfront location allows barefoot dining with sand between your toes. Open 11 AM - 11 PM daily, peak times 1 PM and 8 PM. Regular water taxi service from Skiathos Town harbor.

La Luna (Achladies Heights 23, +30 24270 49420) combines spectacular bay views with sophisticated international cuisine. Their tasting menu changes monthly, highlighting seasonal ingredients through Mediterranean-Asian fusion. Smart casual dress requested for dinner service. Reservations required one week ahead. Private parking available, or €15 taxi from town.

Inland Villages

Platanos (Evangelistria Monastery Road 12, +30 24270 49150) occupies a restored olive press, serving traditional dishes with historical context. Their hand-rolled pasta with rooster sauce follows a 19th-century recipe. Mountain views complement rustic elegance. Dinner only, 6 PM - 10 PM, closed Tuesdays. Advance booking essential during religious festivals.

Time-worn stone walls embrace diners at To Spiti (Upper Village Square 8, +30 24270 49230), where grandmother's recipes meet contemporary presentation. Their seasonal tasting menus celebrate local ingredients through traditional techniques. The intimate setting accommodates only twenty guests per evening. Reservations required two days ahead. Accessible via evening shuttle service from major hotels.

6.3 Local Produce and Markets

Spring mornings reveal Skiathos's agricultural soul at the Central Market Square (Papadiamantis Street 45), where generations of island farmers gather to sell their seasonal bounty. The market pulses with life every Tuesday and Friday from dawn until 2 PM, transforming the heart of Skiathos Town into a vibrant celebration of local produce.

Early April brings the first wild asparagus, carefully gathered from mountain slopes by knowing eyes. Market vendor Maria Dimitriou (Stall 12) continues her family's tradition of foraging wild greens, offering mysterious bundles of herbs that grow nowhere else on Earth. Her knowledge of cooking preparations comes free with every purchase, passed down through four generations of Skiathian women.

The island's unique microclimate nurtures exceptional citrus fruits. The protected valleys around Troulos village produce bergamot oranges with intense aromatic oils, prized by local distillers. Visit the Citrus Grove Cooperative (Troulos Valley Road 23, +30 24270 49670) to sample these distinctive fruits. Their small shop opens daily from 9 AM to 6 PM, offering preserves and liqueurs made from heritage citrus varieties.

Olive cultivation shapes both landscape and culture. The Ancient Olive Grove (Evangelistria Road 78) maintains trees over 500 years old, still producing exceptional oil. Traditional pressing demonstrations occur every Wednesday morning from October through December. The adjacent tasting room (open 10 AM - 4 PM) explains how soil composition creates unique flavor profiles in different grove sections.

Summer markets overflow with small, intensely flavored tomatoes grown in the mineral-rich soil of abandoned terraces. Local farmer Yannis Stavrou (Market Stall 7) specializes in forgotten varieties passed down through island families. His Thursday morning produce stand transforms simple ingredients into educational experiences, explaining how traditional growing methods enhance natural flavors.

The Honey House (Mountain Road 156, +30 24270 49445) reveals how elevation changes influence honey production. Their observation hives demonstrate how bees create distinct honey varieties from pine forest, wild thyme, and spring wildflowers. Tasting sessions run daily at 11 AM and 3 PM, requiring advance booking during summer months. Take bus route 7 to the Monastery stop, then walk 10 minutes uphill.

Skiathos's fishing heritage lives at the Morning Fish Market (Old Port, opposite ferry terminal). Arriving before 7 AM rewards early risers with the spectacle of boats returning laden with night catches. Local restaurants bid for premium fish, but individual buyers find excellent values after commercial sales conclude around 8 AM. The adjacent Fish Monger's

Association office provides sustainable fishing guides and cooking tips.

Traditional cheese production continues in the island's mountain villages. The Dairy Collective (Upper Village Square 12, +30 24270 49890) makes small batches of mizithra cheese using methods unchanged for centuries. Morning visits might catch the cheese-making process in action. Their shop opens whenever production allows, typically 10 AM - 2 PM, offering samples and detailed explanations of aging techniques.

September transforms the island as grape harvest begins. Small family vineyards welcome visitors during this period. The Moschovis Vineyard (Valley Road 234, +30 24270 49780) maintains traditional pressing equipment, offering tours and tastings by appointment. Their unique red variety, adapted to Skiathos's maritime climate, produces distinctively mineral wines.

The Women's Agricultural Cooperative (Central Market Building, Second Floor) preserves traditional food preservation techniques. Their kitchen transforms seasonal excesses into remarkable preserves - bitter orange marmalade, pine honey with walnuts, and tomato paste dried in mountain air. Workshop participation requires advance booking through their website.

Year-round, the Organic Farmers' Showcase (Indoor Market Hall, Stalls 15-20) highlights sustainable agriculture. Six farming families display chemical-free produce grown using heritage methods. Their collective approach maintains consistent supply while supporting traditional farming practices. Open Monday through Saturday, 8 AM - 2 PM.

Winter reveals another agricultural dimension as olive harvest dominates island life. The Community Oil Press (Industrial Zone 5, +30 24270 49560) welcomes visitors during pressing season. Morning visits include detailed explanations of extraction methods and their effects on oil quality. Free tastings help develop appreciation for subtle differences between grove locations.

Understanding Skiathos's agricultural calendar enriches any visit. Spring wild greens give way to summer vegetables, autumn fruits, and winter olives. Each season brings unique flavors impossible to find elsewhere, created by the island's particular combination of soil, climate, and traditional farming wisdom. These products, grown on small family plots and ancient terraces, carry stories of land and people in every bite.

6.4 Cooking Classes and Food Experiences

Skiathian kitchens open their doors through intimate cooking experiences, revealing culinary secrets passed down through generations. These hands-on classes transform visitors into temporary island residents, connecting them with local food traditions through every sense.

Maria's Traditional Kitchen (Old Town Square 34, +30 24270 49890) offers the island's most comprehensive cooking program. This converted 19th-century home hosts maximum six students per class, ensuring personal attention. Maria Nikolaidou, a former restaurant chef turned instructor, structures lessons around seasonal ingredients and traditional techniques. Morning sessions begin with visits to her favored market vendors, teaching students how to select optimal produce and fish.

The three-hour classes progress through multiple dishes, emphasizing fundamental Skiathian cooking methods. Students master essential skills like properly cleaning fresh squid, hand-rolling phyllo dough, and identifying perfect ripeness in local vegetables. Maria explains how island geography influenced cooking techniques - why certain dishes developed in mountain villages versus coastal areas. Classes run Monday through Friday, 10 AM - 1 PM, requiring reservation three days ahead.

Olive Grove Experience (Kanapitsa Road 78, +30 24270 49560) specializes in olive-based cuisine. Owner Dimitris Alexiou maintains his family's century-old grove, teaching traditional cultivation methods alongside cooking techniques. Full-day experiences begin with olive harvesting (seasonal), followed by pressing demonstrations and cooking sessions. Students learn multiple preparations - from simple olive bread to complex olive-based sauces. The intimate setting accommodates four participants, running Wednesday and Saturday, 9 AM - 4 PM.

The Fisherman's Kitchen (Harbor Front 56, +30 24270 49770) provides unique seafood-focused instruction. Third-generation fisherman Yannis Stavros teaches traditional fish preparation methods passed down through island families. Morning sessions start at 6 AM, accompanying Yannis to select fresh catch from returning boats. Students learn scaling, gutting, and filleting techniques before moving to cooking methods. The four-hour experience concludes with lunch overlooking the harbor. Available Tuesday and Friday, advance booking essential.

Wine and Cuisine Workshop (Troulos Valley 23, +30 24270 49880) combines cooking instruction with wine education. Sommelier Elena Papadopoulos pairs local wines with traditional recipes, explaining how island varietals complement specific dishes. The five-hour experience includes vineyard tours, wine tasting, and hands-on cooking instruction. Classes maintain intimate eight-person maximum, operating Thursday through Sunday, 2 PM - 7 PM.

Advanced skill development finds its home at Chef's Table Skiathos (Market Street 89, +30 24270 49990). Professional chef Andreas Mihalopoulos shares modern interpretations of traditional recipes. These intensive sessions suit experienced home cooks seeking deeper understanding of Greek cuisine. Topics rotate monthly - from ancient grains to contemporary plating techniques. Three-hour evening classes run Tuesday and Friday, 6 PM - 9 PM.

Family-style cooking thrives at Yiayia's Kitchen (Mountain Village Road 45, +30 24270 49450). Grandmother Eleni Dimitriou opens her traditional home kitchen, teaching authentic family recipes unchanged for generations. Students work at wooden tables wearing hand-sewn aprons, learning techniques through stories and hands-on practice. The six-hour experience includes coffee breaks featuring homemade sweets. Available Monday and Thursday, 10 AM - 4 PM.

Seasonal specialties emerge through focused workshops at the Culinary Institute (Central Market Building, Second Floor, +30 24270 49340). Easter brings lessons in traditional bread making, while autumn sessions feature preserve preparation. Guest instructors from island families share closely guarded recipes. Two-hour specialized classes accommodate twelve students, scheduled monthly based on seasonal ingredients.

Private instruction adds flexibility through Custom Cooking Skiathos (Mobile Service, +30 24270 49220). Instructors travel to rental villas or apartments, tailoring lessons to specific interests. These personalized sessions particularly suit families or small groups, allowing children's participation. Minimum three-hour booking required, available daily with 48-hour notice.

Vegetarian traditions shine at Green Kitchen Skiathos (Garden Street 67, +30 24270 49660). Chef Sofia Antoniadou demonstrates how island cuisine naturally embraces plant-based cooking. Students learn traditional preparations of wild greens, legumes, and grains. The garden setting provides direct connection to ingredients. Three-hour morning classes run Wednesday and Sunday, 9 AM - 12 PM.

Each cooking experience extends beyond mere recipe instruction, weaving together food, culture, and island history. Students leave understanding not just how to prepare dishes, but why specific techniques developed and how they connect to Skiathos's broader cultural heritage. These kitchen lessons become windows into island life, creating memories that last far longer than the meals themselves.

6.5 Wine and Spirit Tasting Opportunities

Hidden valleys between Skiathos's pine-covered hills shelter small vineyards where ancient traditions merge with modern winemaking innovation. These intimate estates produce distinctive wines shaped by the island's unique maritime climate and mineral-rich soils.

Askeli Wines (Valley Road 123, +30 24270 49780) stands as the island's premier wine producer. Their ten-hectare estate specializes in indigenous grape varieties, particularly the rare Skiathitiko red grape found nowhere else in Greece. Morning tours begin at their restored 19th-century winery building, where original granite pressing basins still see seasonal use. Tastings occur in a glass-walled room overlooking the vineyards, expertly guided by resident sommelier Elena Papadopoulos. Open Tuesday through Sunday, 10 AM - 6 PM, with advance booking required for tours.

The traditional spirit of tsipouro finds its highest expression at Monastiri Distillery (Evangelistria Road 45, +30 24270 49670). Third-generation distiller Yannis Apostolou maintains copper stills handed down through his family, producing small batches of this potent grape-based spirit. October brings the annual distillation season, when visitors can witness the entire process from crushed grapes to final spirit. Year-round tastings include food pairings designed to complement tsipouro's complex aromatics. Tours available Monday through Friday, 11 AM - 4 PM.

Maritime influences shape wines at Coastal Vineyards (Kanapitsa Peninsula 89, +30 24270 49890). Their terraced slopes catch afternoon sea breezes, creating perfect conditions for aromatic white varieties. The innovative gravity-flow winery combines traditional methods with modern temperature control. Evening tastings on their sunset terrace pair wines with local cheeses and seafood. Vineyard walks explain how proximity to the sea affects viticulture. Open daily 3 PM - sunset, reservations recommended.

The Wine & Spirit Museum (Old Market Square 56, +30 24270 49560) chronicles Skiathos's drinking culture through artifacts and tastings. Their collection includes amphora fragments from ancient shipwrecks and nineteenth-century winemaking tools. Daily tastings feature vertical flights of aged tsipouro, demonstrating how traditional spirits evolve over time. Special evening sessions explore food and wine pairing principles. Open Tuesday through Sunday, 10 AM - 8 PM.

Mountain viticulture reveals its secrets at Highland Estate (Northern Valley 234, +30 24270 49440). Owner Maria Dimitriou maintains steep vineyard terraces using traditional dry-stone walling techniques. Their signature wine blends indigenous white varieties with wild mountain herbs, creating unique aromatic profiles. Weekend workshops combine vineyard maintenance lessons with wine appreciation. Tours operate Saturday and Sunday, 9 AM - 2 PM, including traditional mountain lunch.

Modern approaches shine at New Wave Wines (Industrial Zone 12, +30 24270 49330). Young winemaker Andreas Nikolaou experiments with temperature-controlled fermentation and innovative blending. Their contemporary tasting room features digital aroma recognition stations and interactive soil composition displays. Monthly masterclasses explore specific aspects of modern winemaking. Daily tours and tastings available 12 PM - 8 PM.

The Women's Wine Cooperative (Village Square 78, +30 24270 49220) preserves traditional female winemaking knowledge. Their small production focuses on ancient sweet wine styles, including sun-dried grape varieties. Afternoon tastings demonstrate traditional serving customs and food pairings. The attached shop sells local wine-based preserves and marinades. Open Wednesday through Sunday, 2 PM - 7 PM.

Sustainable practices dominate at Bio Vineyards (Eastern Valley 167, +30 24270 49110). This organic estate uses traditional pest control methods and hand harvesting. Their natural wine program minimizes intervention, creating distinctive expressions of island terroir. Morning tours explain biodynamic vineyard management, while afternoon tastings explore natural wine characteristics. Visits by appointment only, Tuesday through Saturday.

Spirit innovation continues at Modern Distillery (Port Road 90, +30 24270 49990). Master distiller Dimitris Stavros creates contemporary interpretations of traditional drinks. Their laboratory-like tasting room offers comparative tastings of classical and modern spirits. Monthly cocktail workshops demonstrate creative uses of local ingredients. Open daily 4 PM - 10 PM, workshops require advance booking.

Every sip of Skiathian wine and spirits tells stories of sun, sea, and soil. These bottles capture the essence of island life - from morning mists rolling over mountain vineyards to evening light gilding coastal terraces. Whether sampling centuries-old recipes or innovative new productions, tasting experiences connect visitors with the island's liquid heritage.

Chapter 7: Cultural Immersion

7.1 Religious Heritage and Monastery Tours

The monasteries of Skiathos rise from pine-clad hills like anchors of island spirituality, their stone walls holding centuries of devotion and cultural memory. These sacred spaces continue shaping island life through daily rhythms of prayer and tradition.

Evangelistria Monastery crowns the northern heights (Monastery Road 1, +30 24270 49550), standing as Skiathos's most significant religious monument. Built in 1794, its robust walls and defensive towers reflect turbulent times when monasteries served as both spiritual centers and refuges. Reaching Evangelistria requires a 20-minute drive from Skiathos Town along a well-maintained mountain road. Morning bus service runs hourly from the central station, with the first departure at 8 AM.

The monastery complex reveals architectural brilliance through its cruciform church design. Massive cypress doors open into a sanctuary where golden light filters through ancient olive oil lamps, illuminating exceptional iconography. The central dome, supported by graceful arches, creates perfect acoustics for Byzantine chant. Morning services (7 AM - 8:30 AM) welcome respectful visitors, though photography remains prohibited during worship.

Proper dress proves essential - the monastery provides wrap-around skirts and shoulder coverings at the entrance for those needing them. Men must wear long trousers, while women's dresses should reach below knees. The resident monks appreciate quiet voices and mindful behavior, especially near the church and cells.

Evangelistria's museum (open 9 AM - 5 PM, closed Mondays) houses remarkable treasures. Glass cases protect hand-written manuscripts dating to the 16th century, while elaborately embroidered vestments demonstrate exceptional craftsmanship. The monastery's role in Greek independence shines through displays of the first Greek flag, woven by nuns in 1807.

Higher on the mountain, Panagia Kounistra Monastery (Mountain Path 45, +30 24270 49670) preserves more intimate traditions. According to legend, monks discovered its miraculous icon swaying in a pine tree - hence the name "kounistra" (swinging). The small 17th-century church contains exceptional frescoes depicting this discovery. Access requires a challenging 45-minute hike from Evangelistria or arranged transport through local tour operators.

Kounistra's annual festival (November 21) transforms the quiet monastery into a center of island celebration. Hundreds of pilgrims climb the mountain path, carrying offerings and singing traditional hymns. The evening service, illuminated solely by beeswax candles, creates an atmosphere of timeless devotion.

The ruins of Kechria Monastery (North Coast Path, unmarked) tell different stories. Abandoned in the 18th century, its weathered walls demonstrate early monastic architecture. Reaching these ruins demands a guided hike (contact Mountain Guides Association, +30 24270 49780) along the rugged northern coast. The site's remote location and dramatic setting above crashing waves reward adventurous visitors with profound solitude.

Modern monastic life continues at Panagia Eikonistria (Valley Road 89, +30 24270 49440), where nuns maintain traditional handicrafts. Their workshop produces exceptional embroidery and icon paintings using centuries-old techniques. Morning visitors might hear melodic chanting floating from the small church while watching skilled hands create intricate designs. The convent shop offers unique religious items, with proceeds supporting restoration work.

Each monastery maintains distinct visiting hours and customs. Evangelistria welcomes visitors daily 9 AM - 6 PM (summer) and 9 AM - 4 PM (winter). Kounistra opens Tuesday through Sunday, 10 AM - 2 PM. Eikonistria receives guests by appointment only, arranged through their website or local travel offices.

Photography policies vary by location. Evangelistria permits exterior shots and museum photography without flash. Kounistra allows no photography inside the church but welcomes respectful documentation of its grounds. Eikonistria requests complete photography abstention, preserving their contemplative atmosphere.

These sacred spaces blend spiritual and cultural heritage through living traditions. Monks still produce renowned honey using methods unchanged for generations. Monastery gardens maintain ancient herb varieties used in traditional medicine. Evening vespers fill ancient churches with the same haunting melodies that echoed centuries ago.

Understanding monastery etiquette enriches any visit. Enter churches slowly, allowing eyes to adjust to subtle light. Move quietly, especially near areas marked for silent prayer. Accept offered blessed bread (antidoron) with both hands as a sign of respect. These simple courtesies demonstrate cultural awareness while deepening personal experience of these extraordinary places.

7.2 Traditional Festivals and Celebrations

The festivals of Skiathos pulse with ancient rhythms, marking the year's passage through celebrations that bind past to present. These events transform ordinary spaces into stages where tradition springs to vibrant life.

February awakens the island from winter slumber with Apokries (Carnival). The three-week celebration builds gradually, beginning with family feasts where traditional masks emerge from storage. Children practice ancient songs, while grandmothers prepare special carnival sweets like galaktoboureko and rice pudding. The final weekend explodes into island-wide revelry centered in Skiathos Town's main square, where costume parades and street performances continue until dawn.

The solemn period of Great Lent begins with Clean Monday, when families gather on hillsides to fly kites and share traditional fasting foods. Local bakeries produce special Lenten breads decorated with elaborate designs, while tavernas serve octopus and shellfish dishes that respect religious restrictions. The day culminates in evening church services where ancient Byzantine hymns fill candlelit sanctuaries.

Holy Week transforms the island through deep spiritual traditions. Each evening brings distinct ceremonies - on Holy

Tuesday, young women gather at churches to sing the Hymn of Kassiani, their voices carrying across moonlit streets. Holy Friday sees solemn processions carrying flower-decorated epitaphios (Christ's tomb) through narrow lanes, while residents shower rose petals from balconies above.

Easter Sunday erupts in joyous celebration as church bells ring across the island at midnight. Families carrying decorated candles process through streets illuminated by fireworks. Traditional lamb roasts begin before dawn, with preparations starting days earlier as men clean spits and women prepare special Easter breads. Communities gather in village squares to share food and dance traditional syrtos steps passed down through generations.

Summer brings the Festival of Agia Paraskevi (July 26), centered around the chapel bearing her name. The celebration begins with evening vespers, followed by an all-night vigil where older women share stories of miracles attributed to the saint. Dawn brings a procession carrying her icon through streets decorated with pine branches and wild flowers. Local homes open to visitors, serving traditional sweets and retsina wine.

The Assumption of the Virgin (August 15) stands as summer's crowning celebration. Preparations begin weeks earlier as churches are cleaned and decorated. The eve of the feast sees families visiting graves of departed relatives, cleaning marble stones and lighting memorial lamps. The main ceremony fills Evangelistria Monastery's courtyard with hundreds of worshippers holding candles in the warm night air.

September welcomes the Wine Festival, marking grape harvest completion. Local vintners set up stalls around the old harbor, offering tastings of new wines alongside traditional island dishes. Evening entertainment features folk musicians playing gaida (bagpipes) and traditional string instruments. Elderly residents sometimes demonstrate old harvest dances, their movements telling stories of agricultural life.

The Feast of Saint Nicholas (December 6) holds special significance in this seafaring community. Fisher families bring offerings to his chapel overlooking the harbor, while boats decorated with flags parade along the coast. Evening celebrations include special fish dishes and stories of the saint's protection of sailors. Children receive small gifts representing maritime traditions.

Modern additions complement ancient customs without displacing them. The Cultural Festival (July) brings contemporary artists and performers while maintaining traditional elements. Open-air cinema screenings share space with demonstrations of traditional crafts. Evening concerts might feature modern compositions alongside ancient island songs.

These celebrations require various levels of visitor participation. Religious festivals welcome respectful observers but demand appropriate behavior and dress. Community celebrations embrace everyone willing to learn traditional dances or help prepare festival foods. Understanding basic customs enriches the experience - accepting offered food with both hands, joining circle dances from the right side.

Each festival preserves distinct elements of island heritage. Carnival masks reflect ancient theatrical traditions. Easter customs blend Byzantine ceremony with local practices. Summer festivals maintain agricultural connections through food and dance. Winter celebrations remember maritime heritage through story and ritual.

The island's festival calendar continues evolving while maintaining essential traditions. Young people add contemporary elements while preserving core customs. New technology documents ancient practices, ensuring their survival. Yet the heart of these celebrations remains unchanged - moments when community bonds strengthen through shared tradition and joy.

7.3 Arts and Crafts Scene

The artistic heritage of Skiathos pulses through its winding streets and hidden studios, where creative expression takes root in both age-old traditions and contemporary interpretations. As morning light washes over the island's whitewashed buildings, local artisans begin their daily practice, transforming raw materials into pieces that capture the essence of island living.

In the heart of Skiathos Town, Maria Nikolaidou's ceramic studio stands as a testament to the island's evolving artistic identity. Her hands shape clay into delicate vessels adorned with motifs inspired by the Aegean waves. What makes her work particularly striking is how she incorporates fragments of sea glass and weathered pottery found along the shoreline, creating a dialogue between past and present.

The narrow streets of the old town harbor numerous workshops where visitors can observe artisans at work. The Skiathos Arts Collective, established in 1985, maintains a communal space where painters, sculptors, and mixed-media artists collaborate and display their creations. Here, Yannis Stavrou's large-scale paintings command attention, depicting island landscapes through an abstract lens that captures the emotional resonance of Skiathos's changing seasons.

Traditional craftsmanship finds its strongest expression in the hands of woodworker Dimitris Alexiou, whose workshop near the old port has been active since the 1960s. His intricate olive wood sculptures tell stories of maritime life, while his practical pieces - from serving bowls to decorative boxes - showcase the natural beauty of local materials. Alexiou's apprenticeship program ensures these techniques continue through younger generations.

The influence of island life permeates every artistic medium. Local photographer Elena Papadopoulou captures the interplay of light and shadow across traditional architecture, while her documentary series examines the changing face of island communities. Her gallery, housed in a restored 19th-century building, provides insight into Skiathos's social transformation through carefully curated images.

Modern artists increasingly interpret traditional themes through contemporary lenses. The Skiathos Modern Art Museum, opened in 2023, showcases how young artists engage with their heritage. Sofia Antoniadou's installation work combines digital projections with handwoven textiles, creating immersive experiences that question the relationship between tradition and progress.

The island's artistic calendar peaks during the summer months. The Annual Skiathos Arts Festival transforms public spaces into open-air galleries, where international artists collaborate with local creators. Workshop opportunities abound, allowing visitors to learn traditional pottery techniques, natural dyeing processes, and contemporary painting methods from established practitioners.

In the village of Kanapitsa, the Women's Cooperative maintains a vital link to traditional crafts. Their workshop produces hand-loomed textiles using patterns passed down through generations. These skilled artisans incorporate natural dyes derived from local plants, creating pieces that reflect the island's botanical diversity.

The commercial heart of Skiathos's art scene centers around Papadiamantis Street, where galleries and craft shops display works ranging from affordable souvenirs to significant investment pieces. The Aegean Art Gallery, curated by Andreas Mavromatis, specializes in promoting emerging Greek artists while maintaining a strong connection to traditional forms.

Contemporary jewelry designers draw inspiration from ancient Greek motifs while incorporating modern aesthetics. Marina Katsoulis's studio showcases pieces that combine silver, local stones, and sea elements, creating wearable art that speaks to both tradition and innovation. Her work exemplifies how young artists reinterpret cultural heritage for modern sensibilities.

The island's natural environment profoundly influences artistic production. Sculptors work with materials washed ashore, painters capture the changing light across the sea, and photographers document the interplay between human activity and natural landscapes. This deep connection to place gives Skiathos art its distinctive character.

Beyond commercial spaces, art appears in unexpected locations across the island. Restaurant walls feature rotating exhibitions by local artists, churches display contemporary religious icons, and public spaces host permanent installations that reflect community values. This integration of art into daily life speaks to its cultural significance.

The municipality's recent initiatives support artistic development through residency programs, bringing international artists to work alongside local creators. These collaborations inject fresh perspectives into the island's artistic dialogue while maintaining strong connections to place and tradition.

Visitors seeking authentic crafts should venture beyond tourist areas to discover workshops where artists actively create. Many studios welcome observers, and some offer hands-on experiences. Understanding the processes behind these creations enhances appreciation for the finished pieces and supports the continuation of artistic traditions.

The artistic vitality of Skiathos reflects broader cultural currents while maintaining its distinct island identity. Through changing seasons and generations, this creative community continues to evolve, interpreting traditional themes through contemporary perspectives while remaining rooted in the rhythms of island life.

7.4 Local Customs and Etiquette

Understanding local customs in Skiathos requires sensitivity to an intricate social fabric woven through centuries of island life. These practices, deeply embedded in daily interactions, reflect values that prioritize respect, community, and tradition while embracing modern Greek life.

Religious observance shapes many social norms on Skiathos. When visiting Orthodox churches, modest dress remains essential - shoulders and knees should be covered. Women might receive a wrap at the entrance if needed. Photography inside churches requires explicit permission, and visitors should note that flash photography near icons shows deep disrespect. During services, stand quietly near the back, observing rather than walking around.

Meal times exemplify the island's social heart. Lunch typically starts around 2 PM, while dinner rarely begins before 9 PM. Arriving exactly on time to a dinner invitation might catch your hosts still preparing - coming 15-30 minutes late shows better understanding of local rhythm. When invited to someone's home, bringing a small gift demonstrates thoughtfulness. Wine, sweets, or flowers work well, though avoid white flowers, which Greeks associate with mourning.

The practice of sharing food runs deep in Skiathian culture. When dining out, meals become communal experiences.

Individual ordering of dishes seems foreign here - instead, people order multiple dishes to share among the table. Waiting to eat until everyone receives their food shows consideration. Leave a small portion on shared plates rather than taking the last piece without offering it to others first.

Social interactions carry their own protocol. Greeks often stand closer during conversations than visitors might expect, and stepping back could seem standoffish. Physical contact during conversation - a hand on the shoulder or touch on the arm - represents normal friendly behavior rather than invasion of personal space. However, this varies between generations, with younger Skiathians sometimes adopting more reserved European norms.

Business hours reflect traditional siesta culture, though this practice evolves with tourism. Many shops close between 2 PM and 5 PM, reopening until late evening. Planning errands around these hours shows respect for local rhythms. Smaller shops might close for important religious holidays or family events - locals understand these priorities trump commercial concerns.

Gestures carry significant meaning. The "thumbs up" gesture can seem aggressive in certain contexts. When declining something, a single backward tilt of the head communicates "no" more naturally than shaking the head. Pointing with the index finger appears rude - an open palm works better when indicating direction.

Beach culture blends traditional values with modern lifestyle. Topless sunbathing, while common on some tourist beaches, should be avoided near family-oriented areas or religious sites. Covering swimwear when walking through town or entering shops shows cultural awareness. Many older residents still observe proper beach attire, even in casual settings.

Family structures influence social dynamics. Respect for elders remains paramount - standing when older people enter a room, offering your seat, or serving them first at meals demonstrates good manners. Children receive abundant attention, and complimenting them appropriately pleases parents. However, asking very personal questions about family matters early in acquaintanceship crosses boundaries.

Coffee culture epitomizes social etiquette. Greek coffee drinking involves specific customs - never rush this social ritual. Accepting coffee when offered, even if declined initially, smooths social connections. Reading coffee grounds, while sometimes offered playfully to tourists, holds genuine cultural significance for many locals.

Wedding and religious celebrations involve complex protocols. If invited to these events, observe other guests' behavior. During wedding receptions, guests often pin money to the couple's clothing while dancing - participating in this tradition, even symbolically, shows appreciation for local customs.

Bargaining, common in many Mediterranean countries, has limited acceptance in Skiathos. Fixed prices prevail in most shops, though some flexibility might exist in markets or with individual artisans. Aggressive haggling can offend - subtle inquiries about "best prices" work better.

Environmental consciousness reflects growing cultural values. Using reusable water bottles, properly disposing of waste, and respecting natural spaces aligns with local efforts to preserve island beauty. Many residents feel strong emotional connections to their natural environment - treating it carelessly breaches social norms.

Music and dance events require particular etiquette. Joining traditional dances when invited honors local culture, but waiting for an invitation shows respect. Appreciative watching and clapping encourages performers without overshadowing community participation.

These customs, while numerous, stem from a culture that values hospitality, respect, and community harmony. Visitors who approach local practices with genuine interest and willingness to learn often find Skiathians eager to share deeper insights into their way of life.

7.5 Language Guide: Essential Greek Phrases

The Greek language in Skiathos carries unique melodic qualities shaped by centuries of island life and maritime culture. Understanding basic phrases opens doors to meaningful connections, while proper pronunciation reflects respect for local linguistic traditions.

Standard greetings take on special importance in Skiathos. "Kalimera" (good morning) sounds like kah-lee-MEH-rah, with emphasis on the second-to-last syllable. Greeks use this greeting until early afternoon, making it essential in morning interactions at bakeries, markets, or cafes. The afternoon greeting "Kalispera" (kah-lee-SPEH-rah) begins around 2 PM, while "Kalinixta" (kah-lee-NEEKH-tah) serves as goodnight.

Local dialect variations distinguish Skiathian Greek from mainland pronunciations. Island residents often soften certain consonants and extend vowel sounds, reflecting the rhythmic influence of sea winds and harbor life. The word "thalassa" (sea) becomes "thaalassa" in local speech, with an elongated second syllable expressing deep connection to maritime heritage.

Essential dining phrases help create smooth restaurant experiences. "Parakalo" (pah-rah-kah-LOH) means both "please" and "you're welcome," while "Efharisto" (ef-kha-ree-

STOH) expresses thanks. When ordering, "Tha ithela" (thah EE-theh-lah) means "I would like." Local servers appreciate hearing "Yiamas" (YAH-mahs) - "cheers" - especially when sharing wine or ouzo.

Practical phrases smooth daily interactions. "Pou ine..." (poo EE-neh) means "where is..." Add "paralia" (pah-rah-LEE-ah) for beach, "farmakio" (far-mah-KEE-oh) for pharmacy, or "trapeza" (trah-PEH-zah) for bank. The response "Signomi, then katalaveno" (see-GHNO-mee, then kah-tah-lah-VEH-no) politely communicates "Sorry, I don't understand."

Numbers hold particular importance. Learn "ena" (EH-nah) through "deka" (DEH-kah) - one through ten - focusing on clear pronunciation. Greeks often use fingers differently when counting, starting with an open palm and closing fingers inward, unlike the Western method of extending fingers outward.

Transportation-related phrases prove invaluable. "Poso kani?" (POH-soh KAH-nee) asks "how much?" while "Parakalo, stamata edo" (pah-rah-kah-LOH, stah-MAH-tah eh-DOH) requests "please stop here" in taxis. Listen carefully to numbers in responses - Greeks often communicate prices rapidly.

Weather-related expressions reflect island preoccupations. "Kani zesti" (KAH-nee ZEH-stee) describes hot weather, while "Kani krio" (KAH-nee KREE-oh) indicates cold. Understanding "Tha vrexi" (thah VREH-ksee) - "it will rain" - helps when locals offer weather warnings.

Social phrases enhance connections. "Ti kanis?" (tee KAH-nees) asks "how are you?" respond with "Kala" (kah-LAH) for "good" or "Poli kala" (poh-LEE kah-LAH) for "very good." The phrase "Me lene..." (meh LEH-neh) introduces your name: "I am called..."

Shopping interactions require specific vocabulary. "Poso kani afto?" (POH-soh KAH-nee af-TOH) asks an item's price. "Akrivo" (ah-kree-VOH) means "expensive," while "ftino" (ftee-NOH) means "cheap." The phrase "Psahno..." (PSAKH-no) indicates "I'm looking for..."

Emergency phrases demand clear pronunciation. "Voithia" (voh-EE-thee-ah) calls for help, while "Yiatros" (yee-ah-TROHS) means doctor. The phrase "Ehi problem" (EH-khee proh-VLEEM-ah) indicates a problem exists.

Religious terminology matters in Orthodox contexts. "Ekklisia" (eh-klee-SEE-ah) means church, while "Panagia" (pah-nah-YEE-ah) refers to the Virgin Mary. When entering churches, understanding "Kyrie eleison" (KEE-ree-eh eh-LEH-ee-son) - "Lord have mercy" - shows cultural awareness.

Regional variations add complexity. Older residents might use words reflecting Turkish influence from historical occupation periods. The local word "konak" (koh-NAHK) for "house" exemplifies this linguistic heritage, though younger generations increasingly use standard Greek "spiti" (SPEE-tee).

Practice exercises enhance learning. Start conversations with shopkeepers using "Kalimera" followed by "Ti kanis?" Listen carefully to responses, noting rhythm and intonation. Record common phrases on your phone, comparing your pronunciation with local speech patterns.

Audio resources supplement learning. The Skiathian Cultural Center offers pronunciation workshops during summer months. Local language schools provide audio guides highlighting island-specific expressions. Several mobile apps now include Skiathian dialect variations alongside standard Greek.

Attempting Greek phrases, even imperfectly, demonstrates cultural respect. Locals appreciate sincere efforts to communicate in their language, often responding with patience and encouragement. Each interaction builds confidence while deepening appreciation for Skiathian linguistic heritage.

Chapter 8: Practical Information

8.1 Banking and Currency Exchange

Skiathos's financial infrastructure seamlessly blends modern banking conveniences with traditional Greek business practices. Understanding the island's monetary systems helps visitors handle transactions confidently while avoiding unnecessary fees and frustrations.

Major Greek banks maintain branches in Skiathos Town, primarily along Papadiamantis Street. The National Bank of Greece, Alpha Bank, and Piraeus Bank operate full-service locations, offering currency exchange, international transfers, and general banking services. Banking hours typically run 8:00 AM to 2:00 PM Monday through Thursday, with Friday closing at 1:30 PM. Summer months see extended afternoon hours at select branches, accommodating increased tourist traffic.

ATM access spans the island strategically. Skiathos Town hosts twelve machines, concentrated near the old port, main square, and commercial district. Koukounaries beach area maintains three ATMs, while Troulos and Achladies each offer single machines. Peak season sometimes depletes ATM cash supplies, especially during weekends - planning withdrawals accordingly prevents inconvenience.

Transaction fees merit careful attention. Greek bank ATMs typically charge €2.50-3.50 per international withdrawal, while independent ATMs might impose fees reaching €5-7. Many machines display fee information only in Greek - learning to recognize key terms helps avoid surprise charges. Some international banks partner with Greek institutions, offering reduced or waived fees - checking these relationships before traveling saves money.

Credit card acceptance varies significantly across businesses. Large hotels, restaurants, and retail chains process major cards routinely, usually without surcharges. Smaller establishments, particularly family tavernas and local shops, might require minimum purchase amounts or add percentage fees ranging from 2-4%. American Express sees limited acceptance compared to Visa and Mastercard.

Mobile payment options continue expanding. Apple Pay and Google Pay work at most terminals accepting contactless cards. Several Greek banks offer mobile apps enabling QR code payments, though these systems primarily serve domestic customers. The local taxi association recently introduced a unified payment app accepting international cards.

Currency exchange offices cluster in tourist areas, offering convenient but costly services. Current exchange rates appear prominently, but scrutinize the fine print regarding commission fees. Banks typically provide better rates than independent exchanges, particularly during morning hours when rates update. Some hotels exchange currency, though their rates rarely compete with dedicated services.

Seasonal variations affect financial services significantly. Winter months see reduced ATM maintenance, occasionally leaving machines temporarily empty or offline. Several exchange offices close entirely from November through March. Bank branches maintain standard hours year-round, but with reduced staff during low season.

Emergency financial services require advance planning. The nearest 24-hour banking center operates in Volos on the mainland. Western Union services run through specific bank branches and post offices, with limited weekend availability. Several island travel agencies facilitate emergency cash transfers, charging premium fees for urgent service.

Common currencies processed locally include US Dollars, British Pounds, and Swiss Francs, alongside the Euro. Some businesses accept these currencies directly, though often at unfavorable rates. Converting money before arriving generally yields better value than local exchange.

Safety considerations shape money management strategies. Hotel safes provide secure storage for excess cash and valuable documents. ATM withdrawals during daylight hours in well-trafficked areas reduce risk. Keeping transaction receipts helps track spending and identify any unauthorized charges - local police require them when investigating financial disputes.

Digital banking capabilities vary by location. Most hotels offer reliable Wi-Fi for online banking access, but public networks pose security risks. Using cellular data or VPN services adds protection when accessing financial accounts. Local SIM cards provide affordable data options for extended stays.

Business districts maintain specific patterns worth noting. Morning hours see optimal staffing at banks and exchange offices, reducing wait times. Lunch breaks between 2:00 PM and 5:00 PM might limit service availability. Tourist areas often feature evening currency exchange services during peak season, though at less favorable rates.

Tipping practices influence cash management needs. While not mandatory, service staff appreciate gratuities in cash rather than added to card payments. Carrying small denominations facilitates convenient tipping without requesting change. Restaurant tips typically range from 5-10%, while taxi drivers expect rounding up to the nearest euro.

Understanding these financial nuances enhances the island experience, allowing visitors to focus on enjoyment rather than monetary concerns. Each transaction represents an opportunity to engage with local culture while managing resources effectively.

8.2 Communication Services and Internet Access

Staying connected in Skiathos requires understanding an evolving telecommunications landscape where modern infrastructure meets island geography. The mountainous terrain shapes signal patterns, while seasonal tourism influences service quality across different regions.

Mobile networks operate through three primary carriers: Cosmote, Vodafone, and Wind. Cosmote maintains the most extensive coverage, reaching 98% of inhabited areas with 4G/LTE service. Their network performs particularly well along coastal regions and throughout Skiathos Town. Vodafone offers comparable urban coverage but experiences occasional weak spots in hillside villages. Wind provides budget-friendly options while gradually expanding their infrastructure.

Local SIM cards emerge as the most economical choice during extended stays. Cosmote's tourist packages start at €15, including 10GB data and limited local calls. Their premium plan, priced at €30, delivers 30GB with EU roaming capabilities. Vodafone competes with similar pricing but adds unlimited social media access to their €20 package. Wind typically undercuts competitors by 15-20% while offering reduced data speeds.

Purchasing SIM cards requires visiting official carrier shops in Skiathos Town. Bring your passport, as Greek regulations mandate identity verification. The setup process takes approximately 30 minutes, with staff configuring APN settings. Morning visits avoid tourist crowds, ensuring personalized assistance with English-speaking representatives.

Public Wi-Fi blankets popular areas through municipal initiatives. The Skiathos Free Network project provides connectivity in main squares, the port area, and major beaches. Connection speeds average 10Mbps, sufficient for basic browsing and messaging. Peak tourist hours between 4 PM and 8 PM see reduced performance as networks manage increased user load.

Hotels across price ranges offer Wi-Fi, though quality varies dramatically. Luxury resorts maintain dedicated fiber connections, delivering speeds up to 100Mbps. Mid-range accommodations typically provide 20-30Mbps, while smaller guesthouses might share bandwidth among multiple rooms. Reading recent guest reviews helps gauge current connection reliability.

Internet cafes, though declining, serve specific needs. The Computer Corner near the old port offers printing services, scanning, and video call booths. Their workstations feature professional software for digital nomads requiring specific applications. Hourly rates start at €5, with package deals available for longer sessions.

Postal services operate through ELTA, Greece's national carrier. The main post office in Skiathos Town handles international shipping, with reliable service to EU countries taking 4-7 days. Express options through DHL and FedEx maintain offices nearby, offering next-day delivery to major European cities at premium rates.

Remote work possibilities expand yearly. Several cafes style themselves as coworking spaces during shoulder seasons. Notable among these, Ergon Project provides dedicated workstations, meeting rooms, and stable 50Mbps connections. Monthly memberships include printing allowances and locker storage.

Emergency communication systems incorporate redundancy. The island's emergency services maintain satellite backup systems ensuring 112 calls connect regardless of network status. Tourist police operate a 24-hour English-speaking hotline, accessible through local SIM cards without credit.

Coverage patterns shift seasonally. Summer months strain networks as visitor numbers surge, particularly during evening hours. Winter sees reduced maintenance schedules, occasionally impacting rural coverage. Understanding these patterns helps plan critical communications effectively.

Signal strength maps reveal interesting patterns. Southeastern beaches enjoy excellent coverage due to direct line-of-sight with mainland towers. Western coves experience occasional dead zones, though strategic repeater placement continues improving service. Updated coverage maps become available through carrier apps.

Business centers provide enhanced connectivity options. Several banks offer secure Wi-Fi for online banking. The port authority maintains a separate network for updating travel documents. These purpose-specific networks typically require temporary access codes obtained from staff.

VoIP services perform inconsistently across different networks. WhatsApp calls maintain reasonable quality over 4G, while Skype video calls might require Wi-Fi connections. Signal strength affects call quality significantly - finding optimal locations improves communication clarity.

International calling options extend beyond mobile services. Several shops sell prepaid international calling cards, useful when contacting countries with high mobile termination rates. Some hotels provide direct-dial room phones with competitive international rates, convenient for urgent communications.

Understanding Skiathos's communication infrastructure allows visitors to maintain essential connections while embracing island rhythms. Each service option addresses specific needs, from casual tourist browsing to professional remote work requirements.

8.3 Medical Facilities and Pharmacies

Medical services in Skiathos balance modern healthcare needs with the constraints of island infrastructure. The healthcare landscape shifts dynamically between seasons, requiring visitors to understand available resources and emergency protocols.

The Skiathos Health Center stands as the island's primary medical facility, operating 24/7 with emergency response capabilities. Located ten minutes from Skiathos Town's center, this modern facility maintains departments handling general medicine, basic surgery, pediatrics, and orthopedics. The emergency room staff includes English-speaking doctors, while translation services assist with less common languages.

Specialized medical care concentrates in private clinics. The Aegean Medical Practice offers appointments with visiting specialists in cardiology, dermatology, and internal medicine. Their schedule rotates specialists monthly during peak season, reducing wait times through efficient scheduling. The clinic maintains modern diagnostic equipment, including ultrasound and basic laboratory services.

Pharmacy networks provide essential medical support. Six pharmacies operate year-round in Skiathos Town, with three additional seasonal locations in tourist areas. Greek law requires pharmacies to rotate night and weekend duty - current schedules appear prominently in pharmacy windows and local newspapers. Many pharmacists speak excellent English and can offer basic medical advice.

Emergency medical response incorporates land and sea resources. Two fully equipped ambulances serve the island, coordinating through the national emergency number 112. During summer months, a high-speed medical boat enables rapid patient transfer to mainland hospitals when necessary. Response times average 15 minutes within Skiathos Town, extending to 30 minutes in remote areas.

Insurance considerations shape healthcare access. The Greek national health system provides emergency care regardless of coverage, but non-EU visitors should carry comprehensive travel insurance. Private clinics typically require payment upfront, providing detailed receipts for insurance reimbursement. Several local medical facilities maintain direct billing relationships with major international insurers.

Common health concerns reflect the Mediterranean environment. Dehydration and heat-related issues peak during summer months, while winter sees respiratory infections. The local medical community maintains expertise in treating marine-related injuries, including sea urchin encounters and jellyfish stings. Pharmacies stock appropriate remedies for these common conditions.

Off-season healthcare requires additional planning. The Health Center maintains consistent staffing year-round, but private clinics reduce hours significantly. Winter months see one pharmacy handling night duty instead of rotating coverage. Some specialized services become available only through scheduled mainland visits.

Language support in medical settings varies by facility. The Health Center employs staff speaking English, German, and Italian, while maintaining telephone translation services for other languages. Private clinics often require appointment scheduling for non-English language support. Emergency services coordinate through multilingual dispatch operators.

Chronic condition management demands preparation. Visitors requiring regular medications should bring detailed prescriptions using international generic names. Local pharmacies can usually source common medications within 24 hours from mainland suppliers. Some specialized medications might require advance arrangements through your home healthcare provider.

Dental services operate through private practices. Three dental clinics in Skiathos Town handle routine care and basic emergencies. Complex procedures might necessitate mainland referrals, though summer months bring visiting specialists offering advanced treatments. Dental emergencies receive priority scheduling at all practices.

Alternative medicine options expand annually. Licensed practitioners offer acupuncture, physiotherapy, and chiropractic services. The Wellness Center near Achladies combines traditional and modern therapeutic approaches. These services typically require direct payment, with receipts provided for insurance claims.

Preventive care resources help visitors maintain health. Several pharmacies offer basic health screenings, including blood pressure monitoring and diabetes testing. The local government maintains air quality monitoring, publishing daily reports during summer months when mainland winds can affect conditions.

Mental health support, though limited, remains accessible. One psychiatric practice offers regular consultations, while several counselors provide services in multiple languages. Crisis intervention coordinates through the Health Center, with telehealth options available through mainland providers.

Medical evacuation procedures follow established protocols. Insurance providers typically coordinate with local medical staff to determine transportation needs. Helicopter evacuation remains available in critical situations, weather permitting, though most transfers utilize marine or land routes to mainland facilities.

Understanding Skiathos's medical infrastructure allows visitors to address health needs confidently while enjoying their stay. Each facility contributes to a healthcare network balancing island resources with modern medical standards.

8.4 Transportation Around the Island

Moving around Skiathos reveals the island's character through interconnected transportation networks. The public bus system serves as the backbone of island mobility, while diverse options accommodate varied travel preferences and accessibility needs.

Public buses run the main coastal road between Skiathos Town and Koukounaries Beach, making 26 numbered stops along this essential route. Early morning services begin at 6:30 AM during peak season, with buses departing every 20 minutes until midnight. The fare structure operates by zones - €2 covers short trips within Skiathos Town, while the full route to Koukounaries costs €4. Purchase tickets directly from drivers or at kiosks near major stops.

Seasonal adjustments significantly impact bus schedules. Summer months see maximum frequency with air-conditioned vehicles serving all stops. Winter reduces service to hourly intervals between 7:00 AM and 8:00 PM, primarily serving local communities. The smart bus tracking system, accessible through the Skiathos Transport app, provides real-time arrival information and crowding levels.

Taxi services complement public transportation, especially during evening hours. The central taxi stand in Skiathos Town operates 24/7, with overflow stands near the port and airport.

195

Standard fares start at €4, adding €1.20 per kilometer. Airport transfers command fixed rates: €15 to Skiathos Town, €25 to Koukounaries. Radio dispatched taxis arrive within 15 minutes in town, longer in remote areas.

Car rental opens possibilities beyond bus routes. Eight agencies maintain offices in Skiathos Town, three at the airport. Daily rates fluctuate seasonally - expect €35-45 in winter, rising to €60-80 during peak months. Essential insurance coverage adds approximately €10 daily. Most agencies require international driving permits alongside standard licenses.

Road conditions demand attention. The main coastal road features good pavement and clear signage. Secondary roads climbing into hill villages might narrow considerably, with occasional unpaved sections. Winter rains can affect rural road stability, particularly in northern regions. Downloading offline maps helps when cellular coverage weakens in remote areas.

Parking facilities cluster around commercial zones. Skiathos Town offers three municipal lots charging €2 hourly or €15 daily. Street parking uses a zone system - blue lines indicate paid parking, white lines mark free spaces. Beach parking varies - major beaches maintain organized lots, while remote locations offer informal parking areas.

Fuel stations require strategic planning. Four stations operate year-round in Skiathos Town, with two additional seasonal stations near major beach areas. All accept credit cards and maintain English-speaking staff. Operating hours extend from 6:00 AM to midnight during summer, reducing to 7:00 AM to 9:00 PM in winter. One station provides 24-hour fuel through automated pumps.

Vehicle maintenance services concentrate near the airport. Two full-service garages handle emergency repairs, maintaining relationships with rental agencies. Mobile mechanics provide roadside assistance through rental companies or tourist police. Tire services operate from three locations, important given occasional rough road conditions.

Water taxi services add maritime transportation options. Regular services connect major beaches during summer months, offering scenic alternatives to road travel. Fares range from €8-15 per journey, with day passes available at €25. Services operate weather permitting, typically from 9:00 AM until sunset.

Bicycle rental emerges as an increasingly popular option. Electric bikes handle hill climbs effectively, while traditional bicycles suit coastal routes. Daily rates average €15-25, including basic safety equipment. A developing network of bike lanes serves Skiathos Town, though rural roads require confident cycling skills.

Accessibility considerations shape transportation choices. Low-floor buses serve the main route, equipped with ramps and designated spaces. Most taxi companies maintain at least one vehicle modified for wheelchair access, requiring advance booking. Major car rental agencies offer hand-controlled vehicles with prior arrangement.

Private shuttle services fill specific niches. Hotels coordinate shared airport transfers, typically charging €8-12 per person. Wedding and event planners arrange luxury vehicles, including vintage cars for special occasions. Custom tours utilize mini-buses, particularly popular with photography groups requiring multiple stops.

Understanding these transportation options allows visitors to blend efficiency with enjoyment, matching travel methods to specific needs and destinations. Each option reveals different aspects of island life, from bustling bus routes to peaceful coastal roads.

8.5 Sustainable Tourism Practices

Sustainability in Skiathos intertwines environmental stewardship with cultural preservation, creating a blueprint for responsible Mediterranean tourism. The island's initiatives reflect growing awareness of tourism's environmental impact while honoring generations-old connections between local communities and their natural surroundings.

Water conservation stands among Skiathos's primary environmental challenges. The island's limited freshwater resources face increasing pressure from tourism growth. Several hotels pioneer water-saving technologies - the Skiathos Princess Hotel reduced consumption 40% through gray water recycling systems and smart irrigation. Visitors support these efforts by reusing towels, taking shorter showers, and reporting leaks promptly to management.

Beach preservation programs protect crucial coastal ecosystems. The Blue Flag beaches maintain strict environmental standards, with daily cleaning crews removing microplastics and monitoring water quality. Local environmental groups organize weekly beach cleanups where visitors work alongside residents. The "Leave No Trace" initiative teaches proper waste disposal while explaining how marine debris affects local wildlife.

Plastic reduction reshapes island practices. Many restaurants eliminate single-use plastics, offering reusable alternatives or biodegradable options. The "Refill Skiathos" program maintains water stations across popular areas, encouraging reusable bottle use. Local markets sell mesh produce bags, reducing plastic packaging waste. These small changes create significant impact across thousands of visitors.

Energy conservation efforts expand annually. Solar installations power increasing portions of public infrastructure, while LED lighting reduces consumption in streets and buildings. Eco-conscious accommodations like the Green Paradise Apartments utilize natural ventilation and smart temperature controls. Guests contribute by using air conditioning mindfully and turning off unused electronics.

Local food systems support sustainability goals. Traditional farming practices preserve agricultural biodiversity while reducing transportation emissions. Restaurants participating in the "Zero Kilometer" initiative source ingredients from island producers. Several hotels maintain kitchen gardens, offering guests fresh herbs and vegetables while demonstrating sustainable farming techniques.

Transportation choices significantly impact environmental footprints. Electric bike rentals provide zero-emission exploration options. The public bus system reduces individual vehicle use, while water taxis offer low-impact coastal transportation. Walking trails connect major attractions, encouraging non-motorized movement while revealing hidden island perspectives.

Wildlife protection programs safeguard native species. The Skiathos Bird Sanctuary provides critical habitat for migratory birds, while marine protection zones shelter underwater ecosystems. Responsible wildlife viewing guidelines help visitors observe without disturbing natural behaviors. Local guides educate about endemic species while explaining conservation challenges.

Cultural preservation complements environmental efforts. Traditional crafts workshops teach ancient techniques while supporting artisan livelihoods. The "Living Culture" program connects visitors with local families, sharing authentic experiences while generating direct community benefits. Historical building restoration projects maintain architectural heritage using traditional methods.

Waste management initiatives address growing challenges. Recycling stations throughout tourist areas separate materials effectively. Composting programs at larger hotels reduce organic waste while creating fertilizer for local farms. Visitor education emphasizes proper waste sorting while explaining local processing capabilities.

Economic sustainability requires balancing tourism growth with community needs. Small-scale accommodation owners receive support developing sustainable practices. Local guide certification programs ensure tourism benefits spread throughout communities. Visitors support these efforts by choosing locally-owned businesses and services.

Seasonal tourism management reduces environmental strain. Shoulder season promotions spread visitor numbers more evenly across months. Winter eco-tourism programs highlight different aspects of island ecosystems. These initiatives protect sensitive environments while providing year-round employment opportunities.

Education plays crucial roles in sustainability efforts. Environmental education centers offer interactive programs explaining local ecosystems. Marine biology workshops teach about underwater habitats while conducting citizen science projects. These programs create deeper connections between visitors and island environments.

Future sustainability initiatives focus on climate resilience. Coastal protection projects prepare for rising sea levels, while renewable energy installations reduce carbon emissions. Building standards increasingly incorporate sustainable materials and designs. Long-term planning prioritizes maintaining environmental quality alongside tourism development.

Monitoring programs track sustainability progress. Regular water quality testing ensures environmental standards remain high. Wildlife surveys document population changes, while economic studies measure tourism's community impacts. This data shapes future conservation strategies while identifying successful initiatives.

Understanding these sustainability practices allows visitors to make informed choices supporting island conservation. Each decision - from accommodation selection to daily activities - contributes to Skiathos's environmental future.

Conclusion: Your Skiathos Journey

Reflections on Island Life

Skiathos reveals itself gradually, each visit uncovering new layers of an island where ancient rhythms blend seamlessly with contemporary life. The morning light washing over whitewashed walls tells stories spanning generations, while evening breezes carry fragments of traditional music mixed with modern conversations.

The island's evolution reflects thoughtful development guided by respect for cultural heritage. Historic neighborhoods maintain their original character through careful preservation, while new structures incorporate traditional architectural elements. This architectural harmony creates visual continuity between past and present, allowing modern amenities without sacrificing authentic charm.

Natural landscapes remain central to Skiathos's identity. Protected pine forests descend to crystal waters, creating the dramatic coastlines that first attracted visitors decades ago. Conservation efforts ensure these environments continue supporting both wildlife and sustainable tourism. The establishment of marine sanctuaries demonstrates growing awareness of ecological responsibility.

Local communities adapt traditional practices to contemporary needs. Family-run tavernas update centuries-old recipes while maintaining essential flavors. Artisans incorporate modern techniques into traditional crafts, ensuring their relevance for new generations. These adaptations preserve cultural knowledge while creating sustainable livelihoods.

The island's seasonal rhythms shape visitor experiences profoundly. Summer brings vibrant energy to beaches and village squares, while winter reveals quieter aspects of island life. Understanding these cycles helps appreciate how local communities maintain their identity through changing times. Each season offers unique perspectives on Skiathian culture.

Culinary traditions exemplify the island's cultural resilience. Local ingredients still define restaurant menus, though preparation methods might incorporate contemporary techniques. Wine production continues in family vineyards, with new generations studying modern viticulture while honoring traditional knowledge. These gastronomic experiences connect visitors directly to island heritage.

Maritime culture remains fundamental to island identity. fishing boats still depart harbors before dawn, though now sharing waters with pleasure craft. Traditional boat-building skills pass to younger generations through apprenticeship programs, ensuring crucial knowledge survives. The sea continues shaping island life as it has for millennia.

Hospitality traditions adapt while maintaining their essence. Small guesthouses offer modern amenities without losing personal touches that make visitors feel like family. Larger hotels incorporate local architectural styles and cultural elements, creating authentic experiences despite their scale. This balance keeps tourism development aligned with island character.

Agricultural practices demonstrate sustainable adaptation. Ancient olive groves receive organic certification, while traditional farming techniques prove increasingly relevant to modern environmental challenges. Young farmers combine inherited knowledge with new technologies, ensuring continued agricultural viability.

The arts scene bridges past and present effectively. Traditional music finds new audiences through contemporary interpretations, while visual artists reference historical motifs in modern works. Cultural festivals showcase both inherited and emerging artistic expressions, maintaining creative vitality across generations.

Environmental awareness grows stronger annually. Local initiatives protect natural resources while educating visitors about ecological responsibility. renewable energy projects reduce environmental impact without compromising island aesthetics. These efforts ensure Skiathos remains pristine for future generations.

Community bonds remain strong despite modernization. Village festivals continue bringing people together, though now welcoming visitors into centuries-old traditions. Social structures adapt to changing times while maintaining essential connections that define island society. These relationships give Skiathos its distinctive character.

Education plays vital roles in cultural preservation. Local schools teach traditional crafts alongside modern subjects, ensuring young people appreciate their heritage. Visitor centers explain island history and ecology, creating deeper connections between tourists and local culture. Knowledge transfer remains crucial to sustainable development.

The emotional impact of visiting Skiathos often surpasses expectations. Many visitors develop lasting connections with local families, returning annually to renew friendships. Others find perspective in the island's balanced approach to development, carrying lessons home about sustainable progress. These personal transformations represent tourism's deeper value.

Looking forward, Skiathos continues charting careful paths between preservation and progress. Development plans prioritize environmental protection while meeting modern needs. Cultural programs ensure traditional knowledge passes to future generations. This thoughtful approach maintains island character while embracing positive change.

Each departure from Skiathos carries possibilities of return, memories of sunlit moments and evening conversations drawing visitors back to explore deeper layers of island life. The island's ability to maintain authenticity while embracing necessary change ensures its special character endures, offering enriching experiences for generations to come.

Appendices

A. Annual Event Calendar

The annual rhythm of Skiathos unfolds through celebrations marking seasons, saints' days, and cultural milestones. Each month brings distinct festivities reflecting island traditions while welcoming visitors into community celebrations.

January opens quietly with New Year's traditions. The feast of St. Basil (January 1) sees families exchanging Vasilopita, a sweet bread containing a hidden coin bringing luck to its finder. The Blessing of the Waters (January 6) draws crowds to Skiathos harbor, where young men dive into winter seas retrieving a cross thrown by priests, bringing blessings for the coming year.

February welcomes Carnival season, transforming island streets with masquerade parties and traditional performances. Weekend parades feature locals in elaborate costumes, while tavernas host special events combining feasting with traditional music. The celebration peaks on Clean Monday, marking the start of Lent with kite-flying festivals at Megali Ammos beach.

March brings the commemoration of Greek Independence Day (March 25). School children perform traditional dances in the main square, while evening processions carry lanterns through narrow streets. Local museums offer special exhibitions exploring independence movement history, particularly compelling given Skiathos's role in naval operations.

April centers around Easter celebrations, the year's most significant religious observance. Holy Week sees daily church services, while Good Friday's evening procession through Skiathos Town creates unforgettable imagery. Easter Sunday transforms the island with lamb roasts, traditional games, and family gatherings often welcoming visitors.

May heralds spring festivities celebrating nature's renewal. The Flower Festival near Evangelistria Monastery displays traditional Greek floral arts. Local women create elaborate displays using indigenous blooms, while workshops teach traditional wreath-making techniques. The month concludes with Maritime Week, honoring the island's seafaring heritage through boat parades and sailing competitions.

June launches summer cultural programs. The Skiathos Palace Hotel hosts the Classical Music Festival, bringing international performers to evening concerts under the stars. The Festival of Traditional Dance gathers performers from across Greece, offering workshops where visitors learn basic steps alongside local dancers.

July peaks with the Skiathos Cultural Summer events. Weekly performances in the Bourtzi fortress present theater, music, and poetry readings. The Photography Festival transforms old town walls into outdoor galleries, while evening photography walks capture golden hour light across historic streets.

August brings multiple religious celebrations. The Assumption of the Virgin Mary (August 15) sees major festivities at Evangelistria Monastery, combining religious observance with traditional feast days. The Wine Festival later in month celebrates local vintages with tastings, traditional music, and dance performances in village squares.

September welcomes the Harvest Festival, celebrating agricultural traditions. Local farms open their gates, offering olive picking experiences and traditional cooking demonstrations. The Maritime Heritage Weekend features traditional boat-building demonstrations, sea-shanty performances, and fishing technique exhibitions.

October hosts the Skiathos Food Festival, showcasing island culinary heritage. Local chefs demonstrate traditional recipes, while food photography workshops capture the art of Greek cuisine. The month concludes with OXI Day celebrations (October 28), commemorating Greece's resistance during WWII through parades and historical reenactments.

November brings focus to cultural preservation. The Traditional Crafts Week sees artisans demonstrating centuries-old techniques in pottery, weaving, and woodworking. Workshops welcome participation, while exhibitions showcase both traditional and contemporary interpretations of island crafts.

December transforms the island with Christmas preparations. The Lighting of the Harbor (December 1) launches seasonal celebrations with fishing boats decorated in lights. Christmas markets fill the old town with local crafts and traditional sweets, while church choirs perform Byzantine Christmas music in evening concerts.

Practical considerations shape event participation. Religious celebrations require modest dress when entering churches, while photography should remain discreet during services. Festival venues typically welcome cameras, though some performances restrict flash photography. Many events offer designated photography areas providing optimal views while respecting performers.

Weather influences outdoor celebrations significantly. Summer events often begin late evening avoiding peak heat, while spring and autumn festivals might adjust timing around seasonal rains. Indoor alternatives usually exist for weather-sensitive activities.

Timing attendance requires understanding local patterns. Morning religious services start early, while evening festivals rarely begin before 8:30 PM. Many celebrations follow lunar or religious calendars, shifting dates annually - checking current schedules remains essential.

B. Emergency Contacts and Important Numbers

Emergency preparedness in Skiathos requires understanding a coordinated system of response services operating across the island. Knowing proper procedures and contact numbers ensures rapid assistance during urgent situations.

The European emergency number 112 serves as the primary contact point, connecting callers to an integrated response center. Operators speak multiple languages, including English, German, and French. When calling, remain calm while clearly stating your location and emergency type. The system automatically transmits GPS coordinates from mobile phones, though stating visible landmarks helps responders locate you quickly.

Police services maintain stations strategically across Skiathos. The main police headquarters in Skiathos Town operates 24/7, reached at 22730-29111. Tourist police, specializing in visitor assistance, operate from a separate office near the old port (22730-21113). Summer months bring additional police presence to beach areas, with mobile units patrolling popular nightlife zones.

Medical emergencies activate multiple response levels. The Skiathos Health Center (22730-22222) provides immediate emergency care. Ambulance services coordinate through both 112 and the direct number 166. During peak season, two fully equipped ambulances serve the island, while winter maintains one vehicle with full crew. Response times average 8-12 minutes within Skiathos Town, extending to 20-25 minutes in remote areas.

Maritime emergencies require specialized response protocols. The Port Authority (22730-22017) coordinates water rescues, maintaining rescue vessels and trained crews. Summer positions lifeguards at major beaches from 10:00 AM to 6:00 PM. The emergency channel 16 VHF remains monitored continuously. Commercial boats must contact port authorities before assisting in emergencies, ensuring coordinated response efforts.

Fire services operate from two stations during summer months. The main station (199 or 22730-22199) maintains full-time crews, while a seasonal station serves western beaches. Dense pine forests require particular vigilance - immediately report smoke or fire sightings. Water-bombing aircraft deploy from mainland bases when necessary, coordinated through emergency services.

Pharmacy emergencies follow rotating schedules. Night duty pharmacies display illuminated green crosses, with locations posted at all pharmacies. The current duty pharmacy number (22730-24444) provides recorded information in Greek and English. Several pharmacists offer 24-hour phone consultation for urgent medication questions.

Mountain rescue services activate through 112, combining police and medical resources. Local climbing guides assist official teams when necessary, providing crucial knowledge of remote areas. Hiking injuries require precise location information - taking photos of surroundings helps responders identify positions quickly.

Child emergencies receive priority response. The missing child hotline (116000) coordinates immediate search operations. Hotels maintain specific protocols, immediately alerting police and securing exits. Beach lifeguards implement water-search procedures while police coordinate land operations.

Consular emergencies often require specific handling. Major nations maintain honorary consuls on nearby islands, reaching on-call staff through emergency numbers. The tourist police assist with passport issues, coordinating with Athens embassies when necessary. Keep digital copies of important documents accessible through secure cloud storage.

Weather emergencies trigger municipal response systems. The civil protection service (22730-25025) coordinates during severe weather events. Hotels receive weather alerts, implementing safety protocols when necessary. The port authority restricts marine activities during dangerous conditions, broadcasting warnings on emergency frequencies.

Snake encounters, though rare, require specific responses. The Health Center stocks appropriate antivenin, while several doctors specialize in treating bites. Immediately photograph the snake if safe, helping identify correct treatment. Prevention includes wearing appropriate footwear on trails and carrying a basic first aid kit.

Dental emergencies receive attention through private clinics. Two dentists maintain emergency availability, rotating coverage throughout the year. The tourist police can connect visitors with current emergency dental services. Major hotels hold contact information for 24-hour dental assistance.

Mental health emergencies receive professional response through the Health Center. Crisis counselors remain on call, providing immediate telephone support while arranging appropriate care. Several private practitioners maintain emergency availability, offering services in multiple languages.

Vehicle emergencies benefit from organized response systems. The road assistance service (104) coordinates towing and repair services. Rental companies provide 24-hour emergency numbers, usually offering replacement vehicles during repairs. Keep essential contact numbers stored in your phone and written separately.

These emergency services demonstrate Skiathos's commitment to visitor safety, combining professional response capabilities with local knowledge and resources. Understanding proper procedures while maintaining important contact information ensures appropriate help reaches you quickly during urgent situations.

C. Ferry and Flight Schedules

Skiathos's transportation connections weave complex patterns through air and sea routes, creating vital links between the island and mainland destinations. Understanding these networks helps travelers plan reliable journeys while preparing for seasonal variations.

Flight schedules follow distinct seasonal rhythms. Summer months welcome daily direct flights from major European cities including London, Manchester, Stockholm, and Munich. These services typically operate between May and October, with peak frequency during July and August. Domestic flights connect through Athens year-round, with Aegean Airlines and Olympic Air maintaining three daily rotations during summer, reducing to one daily flight during winter months.

Airport operations adapt to seasonal demands. Check-in opens three hours before international departures, two hours for domestic flights. The compact terminal processes passengers efficiently, though morning peak hours between 9:00 AM and noon might require additional time. Baggage allowances vary by carrier - European charter flights typically permit 20kg checked luggage, while domestic services allow 23kg plus cabin items.

Ferry services link Skiathos with Volos, Agios Konstantinos, and neighboring islands. High-speed vessels operate frequent daily connections during summer, with conventional ferries providing additional capacity. The Volos route offers five daily departures in peak season, reducing to two daily services during winter. Journey times vary significantly - high-speed craft reach Volos in 2.5 hours, while conventional ferries take 4-5 hours.

Maritime booking patterns require strategic planning. Summer weekend services often sell out weeks ahead, particularly around Greek holidays. Online booking opens 3-6 months before sailing dates, with early reservations securing optimal travel times. Vehicle spaces remain especially limited - advance booking proves essential during peak periods.

Weather impacts affect services differently. The airport's short runway and surrounding terrain make it susceptible to strong crosswinds, occasionally requiring flight diversions to Volos. Ferry services face restrictions during severe weather, particularly affecting high-speed vessels. Winter months see more frequent service disruptions, though conventional ferries maintain better reliability in challenging conditions.

Contingency planning becomes crucial during peak travel periods. Multiple daily connections allow rebooking on later services if delays occur. Many hotels understand transportation uncertainties, showing flexibility with check-in times during weather disruptions. Travel insurance covering disruptions provides additional security, particularly during shoulder seasons.

Secondary ports provide alternative access routes. Thessaloniki offers seasonal ferry connections, while Glossa on neighboring Skopelos maintains year-round ferry links. These alternatives prove valuable during maintenance periods affecting primary routes or when seeking more convenient departure times from different mainland locations.

Baggage handling varies between services. Ferry passengers typically manage their own luggage, with limited porter assistance available at major ports. Airport services include baggage transfer to connecting flights when booked on single tickets. Several companies offer advance luggage shipping to hotels, reducing transit complications.

Seasonal charter flights expand options significantly. Tour operators contract dedicated aircraft serving smaller European airports, often offering competitive pricing through package deals. These services typically operate weekly rotations, requiring careful planning around fixed departure dates. Booking deadlines tend to close earlier than scheduled carriers.

Port facilities adapt to changing needs. The new marine terminal streamlines ferry boarding processes, while covered waiting areas protect during weather delays. Digital display boards provide real-time service updates in multiple languages. Mobile apps track vessel positions, helping predict actual arrival times during disrupted schedules.

Airport infrastructure continues developing. Recent runway improvements reduce weather-related disruptions, while terminal expansions accommodate growing passenger numbers. Priority security lanes speed processing during peak hours, though availability varies by airline and ticket class.

Transportation connections influence accommodation planning. Properties near transport hubs often maintain flexibility with check-in times, understanding connection uncertainties. Many hotels arrange private transfers, providing reliable alternatives when public services face disruption.

Understanding these transportation patterns allows travelers to build reliable travel plans while preparing for potential complications. Each service option offers distinct advantages, creating robust networks linking Skiathos with international destinations.

D. Packing Checklist by Season

Your packing strategy shapes the entire Skiathos experience, with each season demanding distinct preparations. Understanding local availability and cultural expectations helps create appropriate wardrobes while avoiding overpacking.

Summer essentials prioritize sun protection and breathable fabrics. Multiple swimsuits become necessary, as high humidity slows drying times. Quick-dry materials prove invaluable - pack at least three sets of beachwear, including cover-ups appropriate for walking through town. Sunscreen deserves careful attention, as island shops stock limited brands at premium prices. Bring high SPF products, including facial formulations and water-resistant options for swimming.

Beach accessories require strategic selection. Quality sunglasses protect against intense Mediterranean light, while broad-brimmed hats shield face and neck. Water shoes prove essential on pebble beaches and rocky swimming areas. Consider bringing snorkel equipment, as rental quality varies widely. Insulated water bottles help maintain hydration during beach days.

Evening summer attire balances comfort with style. Ladies find lightweight dresses versatile enough to transition from beach to dinner. Men need collared shirts for upscale restaurants, though smart casual remains acceptable most places. One set of dressier attire serves special occasions - island weddings or high-end dining demand elevated presentation.

Spring packing accommodates variable conditions. Layering becomes essential - light jackets and sweaters handle morning chill and evening breezes. Waterproof outer layers protect during occasional showers, while sturdy walking shoes support exploration during comfortable daytime temperatures. Pack several long-sleeve options in breathable fabrics.

Autumn visitors need similar versatility. Water temperatures remain pleasant through October, warranting swimming gear alongside warmer clothing. Evening temperatures drop significantly - include light wool sweaters and water-resistant jackets. Sturdy footwear supports hiking newly reopened trails, while umbrellas protect during increased rainfall probability.

Winter demands thoughtful preparation. Hotels might offer limited heating - packable down jackets and warm sleepwear ensure comfort. Waterproof boots handle occasional storms, while thermal layers maintain warmth during outdoor activities. Religious site visits require modest dress regardless of season - bring appropriate coverage options.

Technology considerations span seasons. Camera equipment benefits from protective cases against sand and humidity. Portable chargers support long days away from power sources, while universal adapters accommodate European outlets. Download essential apps before arrival, as internet speeds might limit large downloads.

Health and hygiene items require attention. Prescription medications should last entire trips plus contingency days, as exact equivalents might prove unavailable. Basic first-aid supplies, including blister treatment and digestive remedies, prevent minor issues from disrupting plans. Motion sickness remedies help during ferry journeys.

Activity-specific gear warrants consideration. Hiking enthusiasts need appropriate footwear and moisture-wicking layers year-round. Water sports participants might bring their own masks or wetsuits, particularly during shoulder seasons. Photographers need lens cleaning supplies, as salt air affects equipment significantly.

Cultural considerations influence packing choices. Church visits require covered shoulders and knees - light scarves serve multiple purposes here. Beachwear remains inappropriate in town settings - include adequate cover-ups. Some upscale restaurants appreciate more formal attire, though strict dress codes remain rare.

Space-saving techniques enhance packing efficiency. Rolling clothes prevents wrinkles while maximizing space. Packing cubes organize items while simplifying hotel transfers. Travel-size toiletries suffice, as local shops stock basic necessities. Consider leaving room for local purchases, particularly during shoulder seasons when unique items become available.

Shopping options vary seasonally. Summer brings abundant tourist-oriented shops, though prices reflect peak demand. Winter sees limited retail options - bring essential items rather than planning purchases. Pharmacies maintain consistent hours year-round, stocking basic healthcare needs.

Practical accessories prove invaluable. Reusable shopping bags support local plastic reduction efforts. Small backpacks or water-resistant day bags protect belongings during excursions. Consider bringing favorite coffee or tea, as specific brands might prove unavailable.

Documentation requires careful attention. Beyond passports and essential papers, bring paper copies of important documents. Insurance cards, prescription details, and emergency contacts should remain accessible without technology. Consider waterproof document holders during beach-focused visits.

These packing considerations help create comfortable, appropriate wardrobes supporting intended activities while respecting local customs. Thoughtful preparation enhances island experiences across seasons.

Printed in Great Britain
by Amazon

62474960R00131